101
GREAT
CHOICES
ATLANTA

Ric Latarski

Printed on recyclable paper

PASSPORT BOOKS
a division of *NTC Publishing Group*
Lincolnwood, Illinois USA

Cover & interior design by Nick Panos
Cover & interior illustration by Chris Horrie
Special thanks to Jan Farrington
Maps: © 1996 MAGELLAN Geographix^{SM} Santa Barbara, CA

Published by Passport Books, a division of NTC Publishing Group.
© 1996 by NTC Publishing Group, 4255 West Touhy Avenue,
Lincolnwood (Chicago), Illinois 60646-1975 U.S.A.
Manufactured in the United States of America.

5 6 7 8 9 ML 9 8 7 6 5 4 3 2 1

Atlanta: A Great Choice

It's 3:27 a.m. in Atlanta and you suddenly have a serious need for scrambled eggs and grits. You're in the right city but exactly where do you go at such an inhuman hour for the South's signature combo plate? You're in Atlanta, romance is brewing, and you would kill for a cozy dinner. Where do you go? Ciboulette, the city's fanciest French restaurant? Abruzzi, just as fancy, but Italian? Dante's Down the Hatch, where you can express fondness over fondue?

Perhaps it's easier to imagine this scenario: You've been in Atlanta four days and hit all the major family attractions—Six Flags Over Georgia, White Water, Stone Mountain Park—but your 7-year-old is bored and you and your spouse have come down with the urban yips. Where in Atlanta do you go to relax, recreate and decompress?

Vacations or business trips to strange cities have a way of turning into humorless remakes of National Lampoon "Vacation" movies when you're lost and have little to grasp at except the typical every-site-but-the-kitchen-sink guidebook. There's nothing wrong with such books and a thoroughgoing index to a city's every nook and cranny has its place. But, for the average traveler, such books tend to be as exhausting as they are exhaustive.

If a traveler wants quick answers to the most commonly pressing questions—where to eat, sleep, sightsee, shop and party— the handiest guidebook pares away a city's marginal attractions and distills the remaining ones into a manageable, well-organized thoughtful selection of best choices.

Here you have it: *101 Great Choices: Atlanta*.

This guide, keeping the visitor in mind, is focused on central Atlanta, inside the city's beltway (the 66-mile, I-285, asphalt collar, known to the locals as the "Perimeter") which, in many ways, separates Atlanta geographically and culturally from the rest of the state.

Atlanta's main attractions—the arts, dining, music, bars, clubs, theaters, shopping complexes and boutiques—are, for the most part, inside I-285. They are what set Atlanta apart and give it the "feel" of a big city. A handful of our recommendations are located outside the Perimeter because we consider them worth the trip.

The restaurant listings include a wide variety of cuisines and price ranges. Taste, just as wine and love, is indescribable and doesn't translate worth a darn into English. If we picked a restaurant, up and down the menu the food is outstanding. Many restaurants were left out. Of those, some are as good as the ones we've included. None are superior. In addition, in a city with as vibrant a restaurant scene as Atlanta's, new venues open almost daily. Invariably, some will be excellent, and you may discover a gem before we've had the chance.

We only listed two hotels: the Marriott Marquis and the Ritz-Carlton, both superior lodgings in impeccable locations. Atlanta offers more than 50 good hotels and motels, in all price ranges. All the major chains are represented and are always a safe bet. Unfortunately, Atlanta does not have a grand old hotel, such as the Peabody in Memphis or the Waldorf in New York. Almost all of Atlanta's historic old buildings have been demolished—but that's a story we get to later.

Atlanta, just as any city, has its quirks, its warts, its "amenities" that you won't hear about from the local tourist bureau. The author has lived in the city and surrounding area for twenty-five years, arriving when flower children roamed Peachtree Street and Underground Atlanta was really underground. It is a city that continues to evolve, a city many visit and fall in love with. We are happy you've invited us along as your companion.

—Ric Latarski

The City at a Glance

A writer for *Sports Illustrated* once observed that "the only thing wrong with Atlanta is that it's surrounded by Georgia."

The writer was in town to cover the October 26, 1970, comeback fight of banished former heavyweight champion Muhammad Ali. Ali pummeled Jerry Quarry into bloody surrender in three rounds at the old Atlanta Municipal Auditorium, which a few years later was mostly leveled and converted into office and parking space for Georgia State University.

Another highlight occurred later that evening: a number of high rollers and city slickers were invited to attend a private party, at which they were held up at gunpoint and fleeced of their money, furs and jewelry.

There was nothing official about it, no declaration in the papers. But that night the "Big A" moved to big-city status. The capital of the "New South" had arrived, warts and all.

Atlanta has always, with mixed success, sought to separate itself from the rest of the South. And evening the score with the North has been a fixation here since the summer of 1864 when William Tecumseh Sherman came, saw, conquered and burned. Sherman's march to the sea broke the back of the Confederacy and the South, but in many respects he only ignited a passion to rise from the ashes.

And rise Atlanta did. Today Atlanta is the cultural, economic, transportation, communications and emblematic crown jewel of the South. It is busily looking for other worlds to conquer and whatever its shortcomings, Atlanta always seems to be the city other cities are in competition with.

Atlanta is a city of gleaming skyscrapers, world business leaders, population growing by geometric progression (greater Atlanta is the 13th largest metropolitan area in the United States), and the host of the centennial 1996 Summer Olympics. It has one of the world's largest and busiest airports and some of America's worst traffic.

What started as a small railroad crossroads known as Terminus in 1837, was, by the time the Civil War erupted, the city known as Atlanta, a major supply line for the Confederacy. It was a prime target, and when Sherman's troops left, the destruction was so complete the city treasury quite literally didn't have two gold dollars to rub together.

Atlanta began to rebuild itself immediately. In 1886 Henry Grady, the editor of the *Atlanta Constitution*, in a speech delivered in New York City, declared the region the "New South"—no longer dependent on agriculture but with a burgeoning commercial and industrial base—with Atlanta as its leader. By the end of the century, Atlanta began to boom in earnest. Then, in 1917, a fire wiped out most of the downtown area again, destroying more then 2,000 buildings.

In some respects, the city has identified with Sherman and the 1917 fire. To this day, Atlanta seems a city obsessed with building, destroying and resurrecting itself. While the city is rich in history, there are times when a native feels as if the sum of that history is collected in the 1939 film, *Gone with the Wind,* not a single frame of which was shot in Atlanta or Georgia. (In fact, it is not unusual to hear visitors ask for directions to Tara, perhaps the most famous historical site in the world that doesn't exist.)

Certainly, remnants of Old Atlanta remain. But too much of the city has been razed in the name of progress and replaced with gleaming, new, and largely characterless office towers, residential or retail developments. The city's constant urban renewal and repackaging of itself makes the Old Atlanta, or visions of the Old South, difficult to find. It does remain, but it must be sought out. Even the Loew's Grand Theater downtown, which hosted the world premiere of *Gone with the Wind,* no longer stands. In an ironic and symmetrical twist of fate, the Loew's Grand burned in 1978.

Despite Atlanta's hard-earned claim to international status, it still clings to the image of a Deep South city proud of its Southernness. It is the headquarters of big-shouldered companies like Coca-Cola, Delta, Georgia-Pacific, United Parcel Service, and Turner Broadcasting Systems, yet continues to grapple with issues such as gay rights or a dispute over the state flag, which bears the stars and bars of the Confederate battle flag. However, Atlanta's conflicted nature, this fractured Old South/New South personality, is the essence of the city and provides its charm. The visitor can enjoy grits and Van Gogh, line dancing or ballet, foie gras or fried chicken, a lazy afternoon or a night on the town.

With a little planning the traveler can fit a wide sampling of these delights into an itinerary. This guide to the city's 101 most interesting attractions will make that easier.

Weather

Like most of the South, Atlanta has hot summers and mild winters. Summer stretches from May to October with the hottest months being July and August. The combination of heat and humidity can be debilitating and there are times when you simply do not want to be out during the middle of the day.

The coldest winter months are January and February, but some of the city's worst winter storms have hit in March and early April. During winter, daily temperatures can fluctuate wildly. When a major front moves through it can feel like Chicago. Three days later you may think it is spring.

Atlanta will usually have some type of winter storm about once a year. It may be an inch of ice or snow and most Northern visitors find it amusing that so little can bring the city to a stop. The best thing to do is simply wait it out.

The unpredictability of Atlanta's weather can give the traveler fits. In summer, dress light, but have an umbrella or slicker handy. Afternoon thunderstorms are a way of life. During winter, pack a heavy coat and a windbreaker, preferably one with a removable liner. Temperatures can range from subfreezing to the low 60s, and it can change with little warning.

Because of its temperate climate, which enables outdoor sports such as tennis and golf to be played year round, spring and fall tend to blur into summer and winter. *One warning:* Atlanta is a "green" city so if you visit in warm weather expect a high pollen count, so plan accordingly.

Transportation

Getting to Atlanta If you come to Atlanta by air, you will probably land at Hartsfield-Atlanta International Airport, one of the largest and busiest airports in the world. Atlanta is home to Delta Airlines and most carriers serve the city on a regular basis. The old axiom has always been: If you die in the South and go to Hell, you change planes in Atlanta.

Hartsfield always seems to be under construction, but that doesn't slow it down. Moving sidewalks and a generally efficient automated underground rail system move passengers with surprising ease. Despite its hectic pace and enormous size (the terminal and concourses cover over 50 acres), Hartsfield does a creditable job of fulfilling its mission.

Airport parking, however, can be an adventure. The lots can fill quickly, especially during holidays. If you have concerns, it's best to just call the airport at (404)530-6725.* There are also a number of park-and-ride lots. Fees can vary greatly so it's best to check the *Yellow Pages* under "parking" for current prices.

Taxis are easy to find at the airport and are usually lined up waiting their turn. The fare to most downtown hotels is about $15.00, but expect to pay more for destinations on the north side.

For car rental rates, private shuttles, or limos, check the telephone book. Rates can vary considerably.

Atlanta is served by Amtrak, and the old terminal at Brookwood Station reminds you of, well, as old railway terminal. The building is over 70 years old and the echoing click you get from walking across the marble floors brings back memories of old movies. Check with Amtrak at 1-800-872-7245 for a list of fares, schedules, and services.

If you come to Atlanta by car, it will probably be by way of one of the three interstates—I-75, I-85 and I-20—which intersect here. All take you directly into and through the heart of downtown. The perimeter, I-285, circles Atlanta and provides an outer loop for destinations in the suburbs and an alternative to driving through the city.

Getting Around Atlanta Unlike Los Angeles, which grew up with freeways as the pavement provocateur of its sprawl, the expressway came unnaturally to the innately slower-moving Atlanta. Given the chance, the natives will still resist the incursion of the limited-access highway. Atlanta has some of the

---

*****Note:*** Area code 404 serves most of the metropolitan area inside I-285 and some parts outside the perimeter. Area code 770 serves the remainder of the area. Dialing from one area code to another is toll free. Presently you do not have to dial the area codes on local calls. As of January 1, 1996 you will have to dial the area code with the number.

world's worst interstate drivers. Some say it's because good ol' boys and girls never learned that cars come with turn signals; but whatever the reason, the expressway, to many, is a hazard.

Transplanted Northerners have brought not only speed to the game, but also the kind of civility only admirable in a New York cab driver. The northern outer loop of I-285, between the junctions of I-75 and I-85, may be the fastest non-NASCAR strip of asphalt in America. Throw in bumper-to-bumper traffic and tractor-trailer trucks and you have an 80-mile-per-hour version of the chariot race in *Ben-Hur*.

Visitors are better off avoiding the interstate system during rush hour, from about 7:00 a.m. to 9:00 a.m. and 4:00 p.m. to 6:00 p.m., but during non-peak times the expressway system is still the best way to get around Atlanta. The speed limit is 55mph, but the rule of thumb is to go with the flow.

Downtown Atlanta can be maddening. The city is not laid out on a grid, and there is a plethora of one-way streets. Streets in Atlanta also have a habit of changing names without warning. Keep an eye on the signs, which can sometimes be difficult because sometimes there are no signs. If you're staying downtown you may want to consider taking a cab or public transportation.

Driving in Atlanta, as in any major city your first time there, is a job and an adventure. The best advice is to ask for directions, double-check those directions with a map (and carry it with you), and get the phone number of you destination.

You will get there—eventually.

The Metropolitan Atlanta Rapid Transit Authority (MARTA) is a combined bus and rail public transit system servicing most of Atlanta inside the perimeter and, to a lesser extent, some areas outside the perimeter. It has benefits and limitations.

For major events downtown—Braves, Falcons, Knights, and Hawks games and major conventions and concerts at the Omni, Georgia Dome, and Georgia World Congress Center—MARTA is your best bet. Trains run about every 10 minutes and from the farthest reaches (MARTA has 33 stations and about 40 miles of track) the ride takes about 30 minutes. The train service is supplemented by buses.

The system may not drop you off at the front door of your destination and you may have to walk, sometimes several blocks, to get where you are going. Fares are $1.25 (as of this writing), but there is a variety of options, such as weekend or weekly passes which could be cheaper depending upon how you plan to use the system. Your best bet is to contact MARTA at (404)-848-4711 for a complete listing of fares, schedules, and system information.

Atlanta is not generally thought of as a "walking" city. However, there are some wonderful areas of town that not only lend themselves to walking but are best enjoyed on foot. Underground Atlanta, Virginia-Highlands and Buckhead can only be experienced on foot. Unfortunately the disadvantage of Atlanta's urban sprawl is that these places are not within walking distance of each other. The best advice is to take a car, cab or MARTA to the general area and press ahead on foot.

Neighborhoods

Atlanta is made up of a series of neighborhoods clustered throughout the city. Depending upon your definition and whom you wish to believe, there are over 200 individual neighborhoods inside the perimeter highway. Each has its own personality and developed independently. In many ways they resemble small towns inside one large city. Exploring some of these neighborhoods gives a visitor a good sense of what Atlanta is about. They represent all types of people and life-styles and demonstrate the cultural diversity of the city. Like Atlanta's seasons, these neighborhoods tend to blend together. We list only five, but they are by no means exclusive, and the city has a variety of areas worthy of exploring.

Buckhead (see separate listing) This affluent neighborhood may be one of the most beautiful of any city in the country. Million-dollar homes with immaculately manicured yards line the streets. The governor's mansion sits off West Paces Ferry Road, and it is not the nicest place on the street. Sometimes it's hard to believe people actually live in these houses.

Peachtree Battle/Peachtree Hills This upscale area is definitely for those who want to be comfortable but not as highbrow as Buckhead. Many of the homes in the neighborhood are being renovated by denizens who bought them relatively cheaply and have since moved into a higher tax bracket.

Virginia-Highlands (see separate listing) This community's center is the shopping and entertainment district at Virginia and Highland avenues. You will see a lot of foot traffic during nice weather, and it could be the most eclectic and Yuppiefied in the city. It has the largest per-capita aggregation of coffee and wine bars in the city.

Druid Hills Located near Emory University and designed by Frederick Law Olmstead, this neighborhood is one of Atlanta's most beautiful, replete with huge gorgeous homes, rolling landscaped lawns, and hundreds of dogwood trees.

Midtown (see separate listing) Midtown is the center of Atlanta's gay community. Many of Midtown's larger homes, built in the early 1900s, have been partitioned into apartments. At night, the streets are not entirely safe. The neighborhood, however, is bordered by a number of thriving restaurants and bars.

Safety

Atlanta has its share of crime but the city is not more or less dangerous than any large metropolitan area. There are places to avoid, but common sense and caution can prevent a lot of problems. This is not a guidebook for personal safety, but here are some tips to protect yourself.

Have a plan. Map out your destination and call for directions. Ask about locations of entrances and lighted parking. It is amazing how many people will park in a dark lot five blocks from their destination in order to save $2.00. *Look competent.* Nothing screams out, "I'm a victim," more than someone who is lost or confused. Victims are usually people caught by surprise and preoccupied with trying to light a cigarette or find their car keys. If you're alone when leaving a restaurant or store, do not hesitate to ask for an escort.

If confronted by a bad guy, you have to make a fast decision. The basic rule has always been to give them what they want. This is still true, and most thieves simply want the money and to get away. Unfortunately, the days of the drug-crazed lunatic are upon us, so there is no guarantee of your safety if you part with your money.

Under absolutely no circumstances should you ever believe what a criminal is saying and you should never go anywhere with them. Even if the person is armed, your chances of survival are better if you take action early in the encounter rather than allow yourself to be taken to some secluded spot. Remember: Your goal is to escape and get help.

Downtown has a fair number of homeless; panhandling is alive and well. If you want to contribute, feel free, but don't stand there going through your wallet because the guy may decide on the size of your contribution for himself. If you do not care to be bothered, avoid eye contact and keep moving. If someone is too persistent or makes a quaint anatomical suggestion, go into the first store and ask for help. The basic rule is: If accosted, break off contact and move away as quickly as possible.

The MARTA system is as safe as any public transit system in the country. Cameras and security guards monitor the stations, but there is always a chance for trouble. Know when the next train or bus is due so you can limit your wait.

Emergencies

Dial 911 if you need police, fire or ambulance service while in Atlanta. This universal number serves the entire metropolitan area. Most of the 911 systems are enhanced, which enables the dispatcher to see the address and phone number of where you are calling from. However, do not rely on this. Try to get the address and phone number of your location just in case. You may think you're in Atlanta, but the police jurisdiction could be East Point, Roswell or Dekalb County. Remain calm and answer the questions being asked. The dispatchers know their jobs, and in many cases help will be on the way while they continue to get necessary information.

Banking/Currency

Atlanta is an international city and will be even more so with the coming of the 1996 Summer Olympics. If you need to exchange currency, however, your options are somewhat limited—

although more places will likely be offering the service as the city gears up for the Olympics.

Your best bet is the Thomas Cook Currency Exchange. The main office is located in Concourse E at Hartsfield-Atlanta International Airport (404) 761-6331 with additional offices at Peachtree Battle (404) 240-0194 and Peachtree Center (404) 681-9700. Call for hours, availability of funds and fees.

NationsBank also offers an exchange service. Call NationsBank Plaza (404) 607-4850 for locations, availability of funds, fees and hours.

Publications/Media

The *Atlanta Journal/Constitution*, the principal newspaper in Atlanta, may not be the worst newspaper in the country, but it certainly is in the hunt. Not the community watchdog or crusader it once was, the *AJC* is a blueprint for political correctness. The length of a story dictates its news value and there are some issues the paper will simply not cover.

Despite its vast shortcomings, the paper does publish two invaluable weekly entertainment guides: the Friday Preview section and the Saturday tabloid Leisure Guide. Both of these offer up-to-date lists of events, performances, shows, and on-going activities in Atlanta.

Atlanta also sports a sassy weekly tabloid give-away, *Creative Loading*. It gives a sense of what's really going on in Atlanta and you are not likely to see its stories anywhere else. The paper's classified personal ads are the best weekly humor section in the city.

The city's weekly business newspaper, *The Atlanta Business Chronicle*, routinely blows the doors off the *AJC's* business section. It is definitely worth reading if you want a feel on the business climate or the latest on real estate development.

There is a variety of other publications and newspapers in Atlanta, too many to list here, and they cover practically every area imaginable. The best advice is to go to a good newsstand (separate listing) and check out the local publications section. Whatever your interest, you are bound to find something that will suit your needs.

Atlanta has television affiliates for all major networks and several independent stations. The cable Weather Channel is located in Marietta, and Ted Turner's media empire is headquartered in the city.

The Olympics

In 1992, with Atlanta being a strong contender, a crowd of 50,000 people milled around the entrance to Underground Atlanta at 9:00 a.m. waiting for the announcement of who would host the 1996 Summer Olympics. When the word "Atlanta" was heard, the crowd exploded. It was considered a stunning coup and the party has not stopped.

Atlanta's winning bid has not been without controversy. Some say the Olympics will be a huge boon; others say the taxpayers will ultimately shoulder the costs. Some think Atlanta will be a great host city and others believe the city will never be able to handle the crowds. Whatever the outcome, the world is coming.

If you are coming to the city, either to attend the Games or just to be a part of the atmosphere, you had better have planned in advance. As many as two million people will pass through the city during the Olympics. Reservations and tickets will be as hard to find as an honest politician. Getting around Atlanta will be a complete nightmare, so expect long delays.

The best advice is to call the Atlanta Committee for the Olympic Games (ACOG) at (404) 744-1996 to get the latest news on Olympic activities.

Holidays

All major holidays are celebrated in Atlanta and this usually means the closing of state and county offices. In some cases stores, museums, restaurants and shops may close. Even among the major holidays there are a few differences. Presidents' Day, celebrated nationwide in February, is observed by the state on the Friday following Thanksgiving, and offices are closed. State offices are also closed on the revered day of April 26, Confederate Memorial Day (Damn right, we ain't forgot!). You can expect parades on

Martin Luther King, Jr.'s Birthday (January 15), the Fourth of July, Veterans' Day, and Thanksgiving.

Local Stuff You Need to Know

Don't be confused by the myth of *Gone with the Wind*. Hoop skirts are gone and Atlanta has buildings taller than four stories. Nevertheless, this is still the South and there are some things you need to understand.

- "Yes, ma'am" and "No, ma'am" are still considered appropriate.

- Food, especially vegetables, is a way of life. You may think the vegetables are overcooked, but Southerners say they're "jus raht." "Greens" can mean collard, mustard or turnip, but you always eat them with cornbread. You never eat grits with a spoon, but if they seem too thin, you can use your biscuit to push them onto your fork. Grits is a singular noun, but it is appropriate to say, "These grits is good."

- In the South, stock car racing and football—especially college football—is important year round. If someone mentions Dale Earnhardt or talks about "driving a low groove," do not jump into the conversation by announcing you drive a Toyota. A native will tolerate your support of Notre Dame or Southern Cal because they figure you don't know any better. If someone mentions the Atlanta Falcons, just roll your eyes and order another drink.

- Southerners don't honk their car horns unless they know you and are waving. Southerners don't signal, especially before switching lanes on the expressway, and Yankees do. One point for them.

- Barbecue is one of the true delights of the South; you will find barbecue restaurants everywhere. But barbecue restaurants aren't like laundromats: not everyone can run one. If you don't smell hickory smoke as you pull into the parking lot (preferably a dirt or gravel one), keep driving. Also, never buy food from anything on wheels—don't trust a restaurant that can move on you.

- Some things are sacrosanct in the South: church, Bear Bryant, Billy Graham, Elvis, George Jones, Vince Dooley, Hank Williams, pick-up trucks, deer hunting, bass fishing, chewing tobacco, gospel music, Patsy Cline, grits, red-eye gravy, greens, catfish, cornbread, fried chicken, fried okra, Jack Daniels, Southern Comfort, American beer, Willie Nelson, barbecue and momma. Mention them disparagingly at your own risk.

The Civil War

There is no way to separate the South or Atlanta from the Civil War. The history of the war-torn years of the 1860s can be seen everywhere. Historical markers identify many battle sites, and you can trace the movement of troops throughout the area by reading these markers.

To understand the South you need to understand the Civil War, and that is impossible because no one understands the Civil War. The one certain thing is that history books maintain the Confederacy lost and Southerners maintain it isn't over. Southerners are convinced that if the shooting started again we most certainly would win. We are better armed, we have our own fatigues and four-by-four pick-up trucks are easily converted into troop carriers.

The Civil War, known more accurately below the Mason-Dixon Line as the War of Northern Aggression, altered the entire focus of the South and, for good or ill, directed its growth for 100 years. Much of the banter you'll hear is good-natured fun, as it should be, but there are still some who are very serious about the wrongs of the 1860s—on both sides.

Ideally, the modern war of words between the North and South is a way to ballyhoo the best of what we are while acknowledging the worst of what we've been. As time passes, the lines will become more and more blurred and faded, but they will never disappear completely. You see, the South is much more than a region of the country—it is a way of life.

How to Use This Book

101 Great Choices: Atlanta is your guide to a sampling of the best the city has to offer: accommodations, dining, nightlife, sports, and other attractions.

Entries are arranged geographically, featuring prominent streets, neighborhoods, and outlying areas. Pick a neighborhood or street and you will find something interesting to do, whether it's sightseeing, dining, browsing in a bookstore, or going out on the town.

Attractions are grouped into ten categories, each identified by a small icon at the top of each entry.

If you want to go directly to the best places to eat, shop, take the kids, and so on, use the handy chart below, which list the attractions in this guide by **category** and choice **number.**

Accommodations
17, 33, 88

Children
24, 37, 55, 84, 98, 100, 101

Dining
2, 3, 4, 7, 13, 16, 22, 28, 30, 31, 38, 39, 41,
44, 50, 51, 52, 57, 58, 63, 64, 65, 68, 70,
72, 76, 79, 81, 82, 83, 86, 89, 90, 92

Entertainment & Nightlife
6, 10, 11, 15, 18, 27, 32, 45, 46, 49, 56, 59, 61, 69, 74, 95

Miscellany
1, 9, 12, 20, 23, 42, 43, 60, 66, 67, 91

Museums & Galleries
8, 25, 26, 34, 35, 47, 62, 78, 85, 97

Parks & Gardens
54, 71, 75, 87

Shopping
5, 14, 40, 48, 53, 73, 77, 80

Sightseeing
21, 29, 36, 94, 99

Sports & Recreation
19, 93, 96

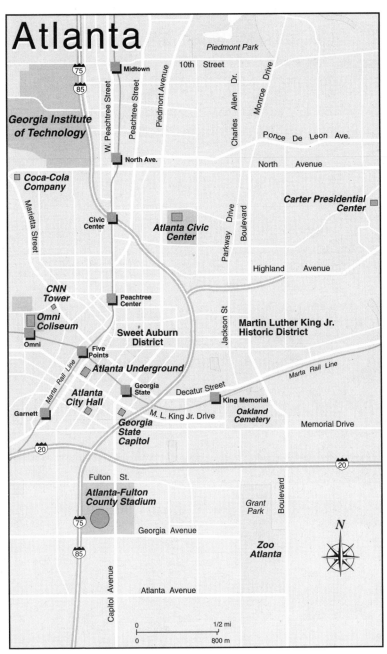

Atlanta

Piedmont Park

Midtown

10th Street

Charles Allen Dr.

Monroe Drive

W. Peachtree Street

Peachtree Street

Piedmont Avenue

Ponce De Leon Ave.

Georgia Institute of Technology

North Ave.

North Avenue

Coca-Cola Company

Marietta Street

Carter Presidential Center

Civic Center

Atlanta Civic Center

Parkway Drive

Boulevard

Highland Avenue

CNN Tower

Peachtree Center

Omni Coliseum

Omni

Sweet Auburn District

Jackson St

Martin Luther King Jr. Historic District

Five Points

Atlanta Underground

Marta Rail Line

Georgia State

Decatur Street

Marta Rail Line

Atlanta City Hall

Garnett

King Memorial

M. L. King Jr. Drive

Oakland Cemetery

Memorial Drive

Georgia State Capitol

Fulton St.

Atlanta-Fulton County Stadium

Grant Park

Boulevard

Georgia Avenue

Zoo Atlanta

N

Capitol Avenue

Atlanta Avenue

0   1/2 mi

0   800 m

Atlanta—Metropolitan Area

101
GREAT
CHOICES
ATLANTA

1 / Premier Nightlife

Buckhead

This Mecca of Atlanta nightlife, which took its name from an early 1800's tavern where a buck's head was mounted, still has about it the air of big game hunting—but these days the hunters are after two-legged trophies. Here, flashy women and flashy men stalk happiness, if not for a lifetime, what are you doing the next three hours? The sprawling neighborhood, whose boundaries have stretched over the years to accommodate real estate interests who love these pricey addresses, has all the trappings of the singles scene and the city's greatest concentration of superb restaurants, shopping, art, live music and nightclubs. Hot spots are too numerous to list, but within walking distance of the heart of Buckhead (the intersections of West Paces Ferry Road, Roswell Road and Peachtree Street) are Otto's restaurant (piano bar, live jazz), Azio's (Italian food with a fusion bent), Aunt Charlie's (tavern, live music), East Village Grille (converted firehouse, bar and rooftop view of the neighborhood), Cheesecake Factory (huge, touristy restaurant with colossal dessert and cheesecake selection), Mike 'N Angelo's tavern; Azalea restaurant (see separate listing), Caffiends coffee shop, The Atlanta Fish Market restaurant; Fay Gold Gallery; Goldsmiths Gallery; Barnes & Noble bookstore, Johnny Rockets (burgers with a '50s attitude), the Dessert Place (spectacular coffee and calories) and Peachtree Cafe (trendy restaurant, piano music). The neighborhood also features a number of upscale clothing boutiques, and, within driving distance, the city's epicenter of shopping: the Lenox Square and Phipps Plaza shopping malls.

2 / Food to Put You in the Mood

Azalea

Were Atlanta Hollywood, Azalea would be a co-executive producer's dream. It's a place to be seen (if not necessarily heard), with the glitzy crowd that packs this edgy, L.A.-influenced restaurant in the heart of Buckhead. The air is hip insouciance: two bars (one smoking, one non-smoking); a two-tiered dining area; glass-topped tables; arty black-and-white photographs of blooming azaleas spot lighted from an industrial deco ceiling of exposed heating ducts and dim recessed lights. On the back wall of the rear room a huge, laminated steel catfish with two-foot whiskers lends a loopy, whimsical air. The menu is a fusion, heavily leaning to Asia and Southwest, with strong Wolfgang Puckish overtones. Azalea's signature entrée is whole sizzling 1.5-2-lb. farm-raised catfish with black bean chili sauce ($10.95). Another favorite is the crabmeat, feta cheese and fresh spinach triangle in phyllo with chardonnay cream ($6.95). You can't go wrong with the roasted garlic, sun-dried tomatoes and goat cheese pizza with basil pesto ($7.95). You'll never order Domino's again. For pasta, try the fettucini with smoked shrimp and salmon with lobster ancho chili cream ($16.95). Another favorite: medallions of grilled venison with jalapeño cheese gnocci, toasted almonds and onion-tomato cream. Azaleas is also famous for its mashed potato concoctions, which change daily and feature blends with tomatoes and herbs or garlic and goat cheese, for instance.

Buckhead

Azalea, 3167 Peachtree Road N.E.; (404) 237-9939. Hours: Monday-Sunday, 5:00-11:00 p.m. Reservations accepted Sunday through Thursday; on Friday and Saturday, come by 6:00 p.m. or expect to wait.

3 / Steak Done to a T

Bone's Restaurant

Since opening 15 years ago, Bone's has been hailed by countless publications (*Atlanta Magazine*, GQ, *The New York Times*, *Connoisseur*) as the place where Atlanta's beef people (regulars include Atlanta Hawks' coach Lenny Wilkens, singer Whitney Houston and Georgia Senator Paul Coverdell) meet, make deals and chow down on steaks big enough for two (try the nap-inducing 20-ounce New York strip or a T-bone so big it's sold by the pound). The atmosphere, at risk of political incorrectness, is manly. Waiters are all male, the decor is boardroom chic, the vintage 1956 Seeburg-Select-o-Matic juke box in the bar is stuck in a time warp (selections include Wilson Pickett's "In the Midnight Hour," and The Beach Boys' "Surfin Safari") and there's a feeling always in the air that somebody, somewhere is about to fire up a stogie. Go ahead. Not only is it allowed, cigars are encouraged (by waiters who come bearing humidors on request). But first savor the best prime, aged, cornfed Iowa beef served in town, char-grilled to perfection (steak sauce is available, but it should be considered a hanging offense). Feeling guilty? Meet you halfway with the hot, succulent, steak salad ($13.95) or red, yellow and green bell peppers, mixed greens, and thick slices of strip steak. Lobsters (sold by the pound), are flown in daily from Maine. For sides, try the fresh asparagus with Hollandaise sauce, and the spectacular sautéed fresh spinach. The Bone's wine cellar offers more than 500 selections. If you can possibly save room for dessert, try the mountain-high chocolate pie heaped with whipped cream. That should push you over the edge.

Buckhead

Bone's Restaurant, 3130 Piedmont Road; (404) 237-2663. Hours: Call for serving hours for lunch and dinner. Complimentary valet parking. Reservations essential.

4 / Where Wannabes Wannabe

Buckhead Diner

Star-gazing is a favorite pastime at this glistening chrome-and-neon faux dining car in Buckhead. Actor Anthony Hopkins scared the willies out of diners when he was seen here shortly after the release of *Silence of the Lambs* (what could he be eating?). When Mick Jagger dropped by, fans grabbed his leftovers as souvenirs. The style is a spectacular blend of art deco and Orient Express dining car decor (upholstered, polished mahogany, transom-windowed booths). But this nouvelle-cuisine diner is as much substance as it is style. Buckhead glitterati make this a regular scene because the food is consistently superb, inventive and served with panache. Appetizers include smoked salmon tostadas with black bean and papaya salsa ($5.95); crispy salt and pepper calamari ($4.75); sirloin carpaccio with mustard sauce, shaved parmesan and crisped caper ($6.50); homemade potato chips with warm blue cheese dip. Best bet for a sandwich: batter fried grouper on farm bread with shaved lettuce and sweet pickle tartar sauce ($9.75). Entrées include a succulent thick-cut, grilled smoked pork chop with spinach greens, cheese grits and black-eyed peas salsa ($11.95); spicy shrimp and linguine with sweet peppers, snap peas and roasted pepper cream ($12.95); soft shell crabs with mixed seasonal lettuces and dill shallot mayonnaise ($12.50); veal and wild mushroom meatloaf with celery mashed potatoes and creamy veal jus ($14.95); grilled ribeye steak with grilled onion and rosemary roasted new potatoes ($14.95). Daily blue plate specials are also offered. The Diner offers a spate of house specialty desserts; the banana cream pie topped with white chocolate shavings is especially decadent.

Buckhead

Buckhead Diner, 3073 Piedmont Road; (404) 262-3336. Hours: Monday-Saturday 11:00 a.m.-midnight, Sunday 11:00 a.m.-10:00 p.m. Reservations recommended.

5 / How Music Used to Be Heard
Fantasyland Records

There was a time before in-line, loop-locked, super-phased CD sound systems when people listened to music on things called records. If you long for those days, Fantasyland Records is the place for you. The store occupies one small corner of a shopping strip on Peachtree Street in Buckhead, but don't be misled by its size. Inside is a record-lover's dream. Counting 45s (those are the little records with the big holes—just in case you've forgotten) there are some 25,000 records to peruse. There are also CDs and cassettes as well but it's the records, real LP's in original jackets, that make this place top of the charts. While the vast majority of the records are used, they are in generally good condition and you can take a good long look before you buy. You can even ask to hear your favorite track; employees will not mind giving it a spin. Prices range anywhere from $2 to $300, but most offerings are in the $10-$20 category. Elvis Costello and Robert Palmer have both been customers, and Michael Jackson once came in and dropped serious dollars for some classic rock 'n' roll. Fantasyland does more than sell; the store also buys and trades so don't be afraid to make an offer. Parking is limited in front of the store, but there is plenty of space in the rear of the building.

Buckhead

Fantasyland Records, 2839 Peachtree Road; (404) 237-3193. Hours: Monday-Saturday 11:00 a.m.-7:00 p.m., closed Sunday.

6 / Tavern with a Brtish Accent
The Churchill Arms

The Churchill Arms is the kind of tavern you might find in any neighborhood—if your neighborhood comes with a British accent. It is not big, flashy or pretentious, but for 20 years has been offering locals an afternoon haven against the work of the day. You can have a snifter of brandy and quietly reflect on the mysteries of the world or lift a mug of ale and sing the praises of John Bull. On Friday and Saturday nights there is always someone at the piano, but an impromptu sing-a-long can spring up at any time. Monday nights at 8:30 you'll find a regularly scheduled darts tournament in progress, and there could be a chess or backgammon game going on in the corner. Pictures of kings and queens adorn the wall behind the bar and a small bust of Sir Winston Churchill hangs over the fireplace. During winter a fire will be burning, and if you happen to be nursing your favorite cocktail, you can almost see the old boy smile. The Churchill Arms does not offer much in the way of food (light sandwiches at most), but eating isn't really the point anyway. This is a pub where you come to forget all the blood, toil, tears and sweat of everyday life; where you come to have a drink in a civilized manner and wonder how you would sound with a British accent. You may be a stranger when you walk in, but you'll feel like an old friend when you leave. Located in Buckhead one block off Roswell Road, there is ample parking in front of the building and across the street.

Buckhead

The Churchill Arms, 3223 Cains Hill Place; (404) 233-5633. Hours: Monday-Saturday 4:00 p.m.-2:00 a.m. Closed Sundays.

7 / Dessert Bar Boom
The Dessert Place . . . a Sweetery

Predating the wine bar boom of the 1980s and the coffee bar boom of the 1990s was the dessert bar boom, touched off in Atlanta by The Dessert Place. In defiance of the exercise fad of the time, the restaurant opened its first store in 1979 in Virginia-Highlands—next to an aerobics studio; in 1981 its second store opened in Buckhead. Since 1979, The Dessert Place has served more than 84 tons of cream cheese brownies (its signature confection) and used more than one million pounds of sugar concocting a spectacular and addicting array of sweets—and giving a whole new meaning to the term "substance abuse." The coffee boom has spurred The Dessert Place's business lately; it serves a delicious cup. The menu varies, but the most popular regular items include Kentucky pie (chocolate and pecan, laced with bourbon), Key Lime pie, lemon squares, apple crumb pie, carrot cake and a notorious cinnamon-raisin stickie that's driven more than one diet into remission. The Dessert Place offers a relaxed, airy setting in which customers can gorge themselves comfortably, free of the guilt that comes with a piece of pie after a huge dinner. Loosen your belt and enjoy. You can start your diet next week, again.

Buckhead

The Dessert Place . . . a Sweetery, 279 East Paces Ferry Road; (404) 233-2331. Hours: Monday-Thursday 10:00 a.m.-11:30 p.m., Friday and Saturday 10:00-12:30 a.m., Sunday 11:00 a.m.-11:30 p.m.

8 / The Way Things Used to Be
Atlanta History Center

A boom town erases a bit of itself each day. Nowhere north of the Amazon Basin is that more evident than in Atlanta which, over the past three decades, has razed much of its cultural heritage in a mad race to redefine the New South. If there's one place to find vestiges of Old Atlanta and the Old South, it's at the Atlanta History Center. Here, history gets respect. The center, on a spectacular 32-acre tract of forest and gardens in Buckhead (blocks from the eye-lacerating Governor's Mansion), features newspaper archives, furnishings, vintage photographs, books and archival collections from the city's rich (but largely obscured) past. They include, of course, mementos of *Gone with the Wind* author Margaret Mitchell and 5,000-plus Civil War artifacts. But, believe it or not, there was life in Atlanta before and after both Sherman and *Gone with the Wind.* Major exhibits at the center include "Atlanta and the War: 1861-1865" and "Atlanta Resurgens," which details the aftermath of the torching from 1865 to the present, with displays from Reconstruction (including an actual carpetbag) and relics from the city's segregated history (including "White" and "Colored" bathroom signs). The Tullie Smith Farm depicts life among the landed gentry in the antebellum rural South (which despite the *Gone with the Wind* image was a very small part of the population). The center recently added a "Children at Play" exhibit, in interactive exhibit of games played for the last 100 years, from marbles to Nerf balls.

Buckhead

Atlanta History Center, 3101 Andrews Drive N.W.; (404) 261-1837. Hours: Monday-Saturday 9:00 a.m.-5:30 p.m. Closed Sunday. Admission: adults $6, seniors and students 18 or older $4.50, children 6-17 years of age $3, children under 6, free.

9 / A Warm and Smoky Feeling
Edwards Pipe Shop

One day political correctness will die the miserable death it deserves and people will once again the able to return to the first—well, second—vice: smoking. Edwards Pipe Shop has the warm and smoky feeling of an old-fashioned men's club. (Sorry, but this is a 100% politically incorrect entry.) It is tucked away in the corner of a little building on Piedmont Road in Buckhead; if you are not careful, you can drive right past it. If you're the smoking kind, it is worth the effort to find, and many obviously have because the shop has been there for 36 years. All manner of pipes, cigars, tobacco and smoking paraphernalia are available here. The wooden Indians in the corner don't mind if you smoke, and if you bring your pipe and want to try something other than your old standard, the pipetender—the smoker's version of a bartender—will fill your stem with a few free samples. After you light up you can sit in a high-backed rocking chair with a cup of coffee and watch the television over the counter. It almost certainly will not be on "Oprah." So what if smoking is bad for you? It helped Churchill win World War II and live to be ninety. Light up and enjoy.

Buckhead

Edwards Pipe Shop, 3137 Piedmont Road; (404) 233-8082. Hours: Monday-Friday 10:00 a.m.-6:00 p.m., Saturday 10:00 a.m.-5:00 p.m. Closed Sunday.

10 / Dance to the Music
Johnny's Hideaway

Johnny's Hideaway is the kind of neighborhood bar you would like to see in your neighborhood. It opens at 11:00 a.m. and offers a fine lunch menu at reasonable prices. But at 5:30, the lights go down, the music comes up, and it stays that way until the shank of the evening has come and gone. The music is a mixture of old-time rock 'n' roll and Big Band sounds from the '40s and '50s. The crowd is lively and the hardwood dance floor fills quickly. Tables and chairs are crowded together, and, while the place seats around 200, by early evening you can expect wall-to-wall people. If you want to sit down, you may have to wait; if you're single, you can expect to be asked to dance (yep, guys too). While this is a regular haunt for the over-30 crowd, do not be surprised to see a good number of younger people here as well. Apparently the idea of dancing to music with words you can understand has not gone out of style. There is no cover except for special occasions when live entertainment is offered, but these are usually advertised. Dress should be evening casual (no jeans or shorts), but don't be surprised to see people dressed to the hilt. Valet parking is available and it's worth the extra bucks. Johnny's Hideaway may be the best place in Atlanta to have a bourbon flashback. Even if you are not a dancer, this is a wonderful place to nurse a cocktail and listen to a musical time machine.

Buckhead

Johnny's Hideaway, 3771 Roswell Road; (404) 233-8026. Hours: Monday-Friday 11:00 a.m.-4:00 a.m., Saturday 11:00 a.m.-3:00 a.m., Sunday noon-4:00 a.m. Admission: free. A two-drink minimum is required if you sit at a table after 8:00 p.m.

11 / Upper Deck Jazz
Dante's Down the Hatch

Dante's Down the Hatch simply does not fit into any neat little category. You could say it is a jazz club inside a fondue restaurant and you would be correct, but that falls woefully short of describing the experience you will have with a visit to Dante's. Walk in Dante's (located in an house built in 1914), and you are transported to another time and place. Suddenly you are standing on a wharf in front of an old sailing ship, complete with the nautical touches you would find on a waterfront in the 1800s. You cross over the moat (watch out for the crocodiles!) to the deck of the ship. You can sit on the upper deck, the poop deck or enjoy the privacy of the captain's cabin. The wharf and ship are littered with antiques that bring the concept to life: clocks from the original Lloyds of London building, paneling from old English banks and a barbershop built in England in 1892. The Paul Mitchell Trio, perhaps the best regular live entertainment available in Atlanta, plays soft jazz nightly. If Dante's has a drawback, it is the limited menu. With exceptions, Dante's is a fondue restaurant, a food specialty that enjoyed popularity for about two months in 1972. Still, the fondue dinners are excellent and, in truth, this is the kind of place that could serve old shoes and it wouldn't make any difference: the atmosphere, surroundings and overall setting carry the day. At Dante's you can plan a romantic evening tucked away in one of the ship's nooks or just enjoy a cocktail at the bar. The owner, Dante Stephensen, a world traveler and former Navy SEAL, is often on hand to welcome guests aboard his ship. If you can only go out one evening and want to have something to talk about the next day, this is the place.

Buckhead

Dante's Down the Hatch, 3380 Peachtree Road N.E.; (404) 266-1600. Hours: Monday-Saturday 4:00 p.m.-1:00 a.m., Sunday 5:00 p.m.-1:00 a.m. Music begins at 5:00 p.m. daily. No cover, but there's a $5 charge to be seated on the ship. Reservations recommended.

12 / Safe Sex

Condom Sense

When Condom Sense opened, people giggled and thought it would be (at best) a short-lived joke. After over three years in business, it is safe to say the gigglers were wrong. With "safe sex" and other health issues confronting all segments of society, the idea of a store specializing in the sale of condoms proved to be of interest to a lot of people. This store, which was opened by a woman, is tasteful and offers a legitimate product that can finally be talked about and displayed in an open atmosphere. The only taboo here is embarrassment: it's OK to go in, browse and see what is available. This is not the back room of the drug store; you will see a lot of women and couples as customers. Along with condoms, the store offers a variety of other items, including considerable free literature related to health issues. The store is located in Buckhead, and the fact that it could open flourish, and no longer be the source of bad jokes and laughter, may finally show we are crawling out of the Dark Ages.

Buckhead

Condom Sense, 314 East Paces Ferry Road; (404) 816-3003. Hours: Monday-Thursday 11:00 a.m.-8:00 p.m., Friday and Saturday 11:00 a.m.-midnight, Sunday noon-6:00 p.m.

13 / Upscale Buckhead Restaurant
Kudzu Cafe

Named after the vine that's attempting to eat the South, the Kudzu Cafe is to native Southern cooking what the vine is to the Southern pine: tradition, with a twist. Here, corn on the cob is split and roasted on the grill. Mashed potatoes come cooked and whipped with the skins. The Moon Pie dessert doesn't come in cellophane: it's a frozen brownie, marshmallow, hot fudge and peanut concoction. The atmosphere is a fusion of owners Richard Lewis and Susan DeRose's two other top-flight restaurants: Bone's and OK Cafe. Clubby (valet parking and an interior whose color scheme and New England air suggest a marriage of Alexander Julian and L.L. Bean) and clever (bathrooms feature window evocations of a southern countryside), the meld works beautifully. Since opening two years ago, Kudzu has become a main drag for Buckhead's beautiful people. They come young and old, but generally well heeled. Mercedes, BMWs and Range Rovers jam the parking lots most nights, during peak power-lunch hours, and on weekends when Kudzu serves brunch. Get past the just-a-shade pretentious awninged portico and inside you'll find the humor intact. Sit at the huge oval bar, have a brew, catch a game on the television in the corner. Best bets include crispy fried green tomatoes (battered, not dusted), a delicious white bean and chicken soup, deep-fried crab cakes, succulent smoky grilled pork chops, and peach iced tea refreshing beyond description. The barbecued ribs fall off the bone but are short on flavor. Reservations are recommended, especially for weekend brunches, when the wait can be 30 minutes or longer.

Buckhead

Kudzu Cafe, 3215 Peachtree Rd; (404) 262-0661. Hours: Sunday-Thursday, 11:00 a.m.-11:00 p.m.; Friday-Saturday, 11:00 a.m.-midnight; Sunday, 11:00 a.m.-11:00 p.m.

14 / . . . Till You Drop
Lenox Square and Phipps Plaza

Lenox Square and Phipps Plaza shopping malls in Buckhead may not be the birthplace of the expression "shop till you drop," but who could successfully contest that in court? Visa, MasterCard and American Express should erect a shrine to consumerism at the corner of Peachtree and Lenox roads, which separates these two upscale, perpetually expanding monuments to overextending yourself. About 20 million shoppers, almost half of them from out of town, traipse through the malls yearly. A day (and an inheritance) can easily be blown here. Phipps (a five-minute walk across the street) is flossier (especially since its $140 million facelift and expansion two years ago). Lenox, the largest shopping mall in the Southeast, has more than 200 stores, boutiques, restaurants, and movie theaters. The best-known stores in the mall (which sprawls but is well laid out) include: Neiman-Marcus, Macy's, Rich's, The Gap, Polo/Ralph Lauren, Brooks Brothers, The Sharper Image, Ann Taylor, Laura Ashley, The Limited, Bally of Switzerland, F.A.O. Schwarz, Disney Store and Banana Republic. A food court includes California Pizza Kitchen, Ruby Tuesdays, Häagen Daz, and a wide variety of fast-food outlets. Phipps (with 110 stores) offers the more upscale Saks Fifth Avenue, Parisian and Lord & Taylor department stores and an assortment of boutique and specialty retailers, including Abercrombie & Fitch, Gucci, Kenneth Cole, Mark Cross and Tiffany & Co. Phipps food court includes Johnny Rockets hamburgers and a variety of other fast-food outlets. During Christmas parking is a challenge. Start early.
Buckhead

Lenox Square and Phipps Plaza, Lenox Square; (404) 233-6767; Phipps Plaza, (404) 262-0992. Hours: Lenox: Monday-Saturday, 10:00 a.m.-9:30 p.m.; Sunday 12:30-5:30 p.m. Phipps: Monday-Saturday, 10:00 a.m.-9:00 p.m; Sunday, noon-5:30 p.m.

15 / Funky Pub with a Blue-Collar Attitude

Mike 'N' Angelo's

Amid the Buckhead glitz of high-energy dance clubs, toney restaurants and exclusive boutiques, Mike 'N' Angelo's is a refreshing, funky dive with a blue-collar attitude and clientele ranging from Generation Xers to older, clearly well-heeled types in search of life's meaning—or maybe just a cold one. There's a difference? Not here. Mike 'N' Angelo's, if nothing else, possesses high good humor. The decor is a calamity of motifs from Early Rugby Trophy (there's a shelf of them along one wall) to a ceiling display that includes a koala clutching a tin of Foster's lager. The bar no longer features live music but has a superior sound system that pounds out contemporary rock, Hendrix revisited, and genre masters such as Sam Cooke. Food is first-rate, served by a friendly, attendant wait staff not afraid to showcase the latest innovations in body piercing and combat boot accessorizing. A few items worth a wolfing: Barry's Snake Bite, a flour tortilla stuffed with spicy chicken; vegetables and cheese flash-fried and served with sour cream and salsa; Angelo's Prized Baked Potato Soup, topped with scallions, bacon, sour cream and cheddar cheese; beans and rice (flavored with andouille sausage); Cherise's Reuben, a vegetarian sandwich of sliced avocado topped with sauerkraut, swiss cheese and Thousand Island dressing; and the Duggan Burger, topped with sautéed peppers and Monterey Jack cheese, served with a side of French fries. Mike 'N' Angelo's has shadings of a single's scene, but unlike many Buckhead bars, it's more of a neighborhood tavern. It's a good place to begin or end your tour of Buckhead nightlife.

Buckhead

Mike 'N' Angelo's, 312 East Paces Ferry Rd.; (404) 237-0949. Hours: Sunday-Saturday, 11:30 a.m.-4:00 a.m.

16 / Grits with Glitz

OK Cafe

The faux road-house diner a few blocks from the Governor's mansion in Buckhead is arguably the city's most blatant manifestation of the storied "Good Ole Boy Network." It's where Buckhead's power elite breakfast or just meet to chew the fat, quite literally. The atmosphere is as dipped in high hokum as the biscuits are in sweet sorghum. Dada art hangs from the walls. Fake leather booths and gum-chewing, leggy "What'll-ya-have-Mac?" waitresses in uniforms too tight enhance the time-warp feel of the diner that seems to have been beamed down from 1957. Yet style doesn't reign over sustenance. The OK serves one of the best breakfasts in town, including fluffy three-egg omelets, multigrain griddle cakes and griddle filet steak and eggs. Egg dishes come with sides of grits or hash browns, biscuits or toast. Sides include bacon, ham, sausage, French fries and shaved onions. The restaurant is building a healthy lunch and dinner crowd with Southern vegetable plates and a sumptuous baked chicken. Other delectables include the six-cheese macaroni; meat loaf and mashed potatoes; and an excellent bacon, lettuce and tomato sandwich. For dessert, the apple pie á la mode is heavenly. The OK is at its best in the wee hours, especially Friday and Saturday nights when the Buckhead bar crowd jams the place. Service can be spotty, but it's always sassy.

Buckhead

OK Cafe, 1284 West Paces Ferry Rd. at Northside Dr.; (404) 233-2888. Open 24 hours, seven days a week. Take out available. No reservations.

17 / Putting On The Ritz
The Ritz Carlton Buckhead

The Ritz exudes elegance from the start, a stately porte cochere entrance where white-gloved, top-hatted bellhops carry your luggage, valet park your auto and usher you into the stunning lobby. Antique oriental rugs, white marble floors and French crystal chandeliers fill the downstairs lobby. Public areas are appointed in antiques and original 18th- and 19th-century paintings framed against the Ritz's signature walls of dark walnut paneling. Guest rooms feature bay windows, reproductions of 18th-century oak antique beds, wet bars, elegant bedside lamps and framed botanical paintings and prints. A signature white Ritz terrycloth robe hangs in the closet. The hotel offers room service 24 hours a day (always delivered within 30 minutes). It is advised, however, that you skip room service and splurge. Go downstairs to the hotel lobby, relax in an overstuffed chairs by the fireplace, enjoy an aperitif and listen to the house pianist perform jazz standards (from 3:00 to 5:00 p.m. daily). In the adjacent Cafe Bar a five-piece combo plays in the lobby lounge from 8:00 p.m. to midnight Friday, Saturday and Sunday (there's a well-used dance floor). Make reservations for the Dining Room, which, by most accounts, is the best restaurant in Georgia. World-acclaimed chef Guenter Seeger produces 7-course masterpieces daily. The wine list is vast and exquisite. Service is brisk (though dinner can take hours). The dinner will take a bite out of your bank account, but it's worth it.
Buckhead

The Ritz Carlton Buckhead, 3434 Peachtree Rd. N.E.; (404) 237-2700. Restaurant hours: Monday-Saturday 6:30-11:00 p.m.; Sunday brunch 11:30 a.m.-2:30 p.m.

18 / Saturday Night Fever

Rupert's

Next door to what's been nicknamed the "Disco Kroger" (a grocery made famous by a late-night scuffle in the parking involving Atlanta Falcon wide receiver Andre Rison), this loud, heavy-cruising night spot is one of the biggest nightclub attractions in Atlanta and the best place for a woman to meet a fella who applies Polo by the quart and does his banking in Switzerland. If a remake of *Saturday Night Fever* is looking for a locale, here it is. Rupert's is the haunt of Atlanta sports stars, including Atlanta Braves' outfielder David Justice and former Atlanta Hawk and local resident Dominique Wilkins. Ted Turner and Jane Fonda have danced here. Rock stars Elton John and Rod Stewart have taken the stage impromptu to sing with the club's 11-piece band. The club is as glitzy as its clientele: the huge downstairs dance floor is overlooked by a mahogany and brass bar in the back, with tiered seating leading down to the floor in front of an elevated stage. Downstairs there are five bars. Music booms through a state-of-the-art sound system, and habitués can watch themselves play the field as they slink past mirrored columns throughout the club. The live music, fronted with top-flight vocalists covering Top 40 hits, cranks up at 8:00 p.m. A complimentary buffet is served from 6:00 to 8:00 p.m. A DJ plays recorded music during band breaks. Rupert's really sizzles when major conventions hit town. The club isn't for the faint of heart or those in search of a thoughtful drink. The energy is galvanizing. You either get swept up in it, or it frays your last nerve. Brace yourself.

Buckhead

Rupert's, 3330 Piedmont Rd; (404) 266-9866. Hours: Tuesday-Thursday 5:30 p.m.-2:00 a.m.; Friday and Saturday 5:30 p.m.-3:00 a.m. Admission: men free until 8:00 p.m., women free until 10:00 p.m.; thereafter the cover is $4 Tuesday-Thursday, $7 Friday and Saturday.

19 / Keep Your Eye on the Ball

Bitsy Grant Tennis Center

If you have the urge to chase the fuzzy ball while in Atlanta, you are in luck. Two excellent tennis complexes, both operated under the direction of The Tennis Center, Inc., provide outstanding facilities for the tennis enthusiast. The Bitsy Grant Tennis Center, named for the three-time U.S. Clay Court Champion and Davis Cup member of the 1930s, provides 23 outdoor courts. Of these, 13 are soft surface courts (six are lighted), and 10 are hard courts (four lighted). Rates for the hard courts are $1.50 per person per hour, while the soft court fee is $2.50 per person per hour. The practice wall is available for free. There is a pro shop offering full service as well as showers, lockers and a concession stand. At the Piedmont Park location (separate entry), there are 12 lighted hard courts that go for $1.50 per person per hour. You can use the practice wall free; the amenities are similar to Bitsy Grant. Both locations are within a few minutes of downtown Atlanta. Neither accepts reservations and play is on a first-come, first-gets-to-serve basis. Court time may be limited if there is a waiting list. Lessons are available at both locations if your game needs a tune-up. Because there are no reservations, and there are sometimes special events or tournaments going on, it's not a bad idea to call and check on availability.

Buckhead

Bitsy Grant Tennis Center, 2125 Northside Dr.; (404) 351-2774. Hours vary with the season.

20 / Birthplace of the New South

Downtown

A walking tour of downtown is a pleasant adjunct to a visit to Underground Atlanta. Begin at Five Points and the Wachovia Bank tower (the original site of Jacob's Drugstore, the birthplace of Coca-Cola). Between Five Points and Peachtree Center (six blocks north on Peachtree) are many of the city's architectural highlights and the Fairlie-Poplar district. Walk a block west on Edgewood across Woodruff Park to the Hurt Building (45 Edgewood Avenue), built in 1913. Check out the marble-pillared rotunda and ornate starburst rosette dome. Stroll west back across Woodruff Park and north on Peachtree to the Flatiron Building (74 Peachtree Street), Atlanta's oldest skyscraper (1897) which predates New York's more famous Flatiron Building. Diagonally across Peachtree is the 17-story Candler Building (127 Peachtree), built in 1906 by Asa Candler, founder of Coca-Cola. It's one of the city's most spectacular works of architecture, with a breathtaking marble and brass lobby, featuring a sculptured bust of Candler himself. Farther north on Peachtree at the corner of Forsyth Street is Margaret Mitchell Square, site of the old Coca-Cola sign, torn down in 1982 when Georgia-Pacific erected its 52-story pink marble headquarters (133 Peachtree) across the street. The Georgia-Pacific building rests on the site of the old Loew's Grand Theater, where *Gone with the Wind* premiered in 1939. Macy's department store (180 Peachtree) is especially stunning during the Christmas season. From here you can stroll down to the historic Fairlie-Poplar district, where a number of landmark buildings including the Grant (44 Broad Street) and Healy (57 Forsyth Street) have been restored to their original splendor. Stroll south on Forsyth to Marietta, where you'll find a statue of the city's father of boosterism, former *Constitution* editor Henry Grady. From there, head two blocks east on Marietta back to Five Points. Not all of Atlanta's old buildings have been razed; you just have to look between the gleaming glass and concrete towers.

21 / History Under the Dome

Georgia State Capitol Building

Under the golden dome that marks the Georgia State Capitol Building are some of the finest natural exhibits and displays of taxidermy to be found in the city. No, we're not talking about those elected officials who carry on the business of the state in the same building; we're talking about stuffed animals. The exhibits represent the wide range of Georgia's wildlife and are designed to show animals in their natural habitat. Also on display are Native American artifacts, portraits, statues and war memorabilia. While the displays may lack a certain continuity, they do provide the visitor with a feel for the history of the state and how it evolved. Free guided tours are available Monday through Friday. There are no tours on the weekends, but the building is open and you are free to explore on your own. Although the guided tours may provide a little more information, there is a definite advantage to being able to move at your own pace. The regular 40-day session of the Georgia legislature is called to order (some might say disorder) in January and is open to the public. The Georgia State Capitol Building is the site of regular field trips for many schools; on weekdays during the school year you are likely to see a large number of grade-schoolers and it can become crowded. Plan to spend 1-2 hours roaming around if you want to see everything. And remember: try not to touch any of the displays—one of them might be a Georgia legislator.

Downtown

Georgia State Capitol Building, Capitol Square on Washington Street; (404) 656-2844. Hours: guided tours Monday-Friday at 10:00 a.m., 11:00 a.m., 1:00 p.m. and 2:00 p.m. Building open Saturday 10:00 a.m.-4:00 p.m., Sunday noon-4:00 p.m. Free admission at all times.

22 / Where the Stars Meet to Eat

Celebrity Cafe

Finding a good restaurant in Atlanta's central business district that's not either over priced, regrettable or a franchise fast-food joint is a largely hopeless task. Long-time downtown denizens know about Thelma's (see separate listing) and they're beginning to hear about Celebrity Cafe, a little-known, spotless coffee shop/diner in the Barclay hotel (in the Fairlie-Poplar district) that serves Atlanta's second-best fried chicken (behind the Colonnade) and out-of-this-world waffles. Thing is: the Celebrity serves them together. That's just one of the restaurant's quirks (not including its name, and a very difficult-to-verify slogan: "Where the Stars Meet to Eat"). The Celebrity is run by members of a black Jewish sect who cook and wait tables in crisp white shirts, black aprons and white turbans. Service is friendly and generally fast. The Celebrity's specialty is chicken and waffles. The chicken comes fried or smothered in gravy. Pick the fried. The waffles are thick, light, spiced with nutmeg, and come buckwheat or plain, topped with melted butter. Either way you can't miss. Every item on the modest menu, in fact, is a hit. Other recommendations include the Ansley Special (fried chicken served with rice, gravy and greens, or with corn and biscuits) and the Luckie Street Omelet (made with cheese and chicken, served with a side of fries). The Celebrity makes superb greens and serves a first-rate breakfast.

Downtown

Celebrity Cafe, 89 Luckie Street N.W.; (404) 524-7991. Hours: breakfast 6:00-11:00 a.m. seven days a week, lunch/dinner Sunday-Thursday 11:00 a.m.-7:00 p.m., Saturday 11:00 a.m.-9:00 p.m.

23 / The Johnny Mercer Room
Georgia State University Pullen Library

The South Library at Georgia State University's Special Collections Department has two exhibits you will not find anywhere else. On the eighth floor, in the Johnny Mercer Room, you can see memorabilia honoring the life of one of the most gifted songwriters of our time. Johnny Mercer, a Georgia native, has no formal musical training yet was involved in the music for 90 films and nominated for the Academy Award 18 times. He received four Oscars for his songs "On the Atchison, Topeka and the Santa Fe," "In the Cool, Cool, Cool of the Evening," "Days of Wine and Roses" and "Moon River." On display is the Oscar he received for "Moon River" and the Grammy he won for "Days of Wine and Roses." The walls are covered with film posters, musical scores and plaques highlighting Mercer's career. Adjacent to the Mercer room is an exhibit honoring the American worker. There are displays and plaques detailing the importance and impact the working man and woman has had on everything from victory in World War II to the space program. In February 1995, William Usery donated his personal papers from 1946 to 1985 to Georgia State's Southern Labor Archives. Usery's role as a major labor leader culminated in his service as director of the Federal Mediation and Conciliation Service and as Secretary of Labor under President Gerald Ford. If you want to feel better about having to go to work on Monday morning—or to get as close to an Oscar as most of us will ever come—these exhibits are worth the stop.

Downtown

Georgia State University Pullen Library, 103 Decatur Street; (404) 651-2476. Hours: Monday-Friday 8:30 a.m.-5:00 p.m. Closed Saturday and Sunday. Free admission.

24 / A Place to Find Some Space

Fernbank Science Center

A few miles east of downtown off Ponce de Leon Avenue, the heavens open up and whole new worlds spread out before you. The newly refurbished and expanded Fernbank Museum of Natural History—the largest museum of natural sciences in the Southeast—encompasses a 65-acre forest, one of the world's largest planetariums, a space observatory with a 36-inch reflecting telescope and more than two miles of nature trails. It's a great place for the family to spend the entire day. The Exhibition Hall features stuffed wild creatures in settings evocative of their natural habitat. There's a replica of Georgia's famed Okefenokee Swamp (with sound effects) and a dinosaur exhibit. "A Walk Through Time in Georgia" examines the evolution of the planet through the archeological events that have occurred in Georgia from pre-history to the present. The grounds, perfect for a stroll on a pleasant afternoon, offers gardens, greenhouses, parkland and an unspoiled forest where indigenous plants are marked for identification. The Planetarium, which seats 500 under a 70-foot projection dome, features breathtaking programs on the solar system, the stars and the mysteries of the Universe. The 15,000-square-foot Great Hall includes an IMAX theater, where nature films are projected on a huge, curved screen; a weather station; the *Apollo* 6 space capsule; a space suit from the mission; and a "discovery" room where young children can "pollinate" flowers and feed artificial worms to mechanical birds.

Downtown

Fernbank Science Center, 156 Heaton Park Drive N.E.; (404) 378-4311. Hours: call for current hours and exhibits. Admission: adults $2, students $1, seniors free. Children under 5 not admitted to the planetarium.

25 / Atlanta's African-American Experience

APEX Museum

Before APEX (African American Panoramic Experience) opened in 1985, Atlanta history was largely white history as reflected in the archives of the Atlanta History Center, which has since expanded its collection to span African-American, white and other ethnic groups. APEX's collection is a more pointed and poignant look at the African-American experience in the city, focusing on Auburn Avenue, which in segregation days was called by blacks the "Negro Peachtree." In its heyday, Auburn Avenue was as famous as Harlem as a center of African-American culture and economic clout: More than 130 black-owned businesses lined its corridor, and several dozen professionals plied their trades from offices on "Sweet Auburn." APEX evokes those memories. The museum's centerpiece is the Trolley Car Theater, a replica of one that ran on Auburn in the early 20th century. A 15-minute multimedia presentation, "Sweet Auburn, Street of Pride," narrated by former Georgia representative Julian Bond and actress Cicely Tyson, unreels the history of Auburn from the late 19th century to the present. Separate exhibits include period photographs of Auburn Avenue, and a replica of the barbershop owned by Alonzo Herndon, a former slave who started Atlanta Life Insurance Company and became the city's first African-American millionaire. Exhibits are continually changing as the museum works to commemorate and chronicle the black experience from early man in Africa to contemporary life in America. APEX has ambitious plans to expand its collection in time for the 1996 Olympics.

Downtown

APEX Museum, 135 Auburn Avenue; (404) 521-APEX. Hours: Tuesday and Thursday-Saturday 10:00 a.m.-5:00 p.m., Wednesday 10:00 a.m.-6:00 p.m., Sunday 1:00 p.m.-5:00 p.m. Closed Monday. Admission: adults $2, seniors and children $1.

26 / Soft Drink Museum

The World of Coca-Cola Pavilion

If you make a list of things that are purely American, then somewhere between basketball and jazz, you have to mention Coca-Cola. This American original was born in Atlanta, and The World of Coca-Cola Pavilion allows visitors to trace the history of this worldwide empire. Almost every type of memorabilia is presented. There are films, video presentations, bottling equipment, and examples of Coke's advertising campaigns. The three-story pavilion is a monument to the soft drink and to the genius of Coca-Cola marketing. In one of its most famous ads, singers on a hillside in Italy warbled, "I'd Like to Teach the World to Sing." But what Coke REALLY did was teach the world to market: Coca-Cola is the best-known trademark in the world. The only continent where Coke is not sold is Antarctica. Coke has even conquered space (aboard three NASA flights). The diversity of the Coca-Cola items in the gift shop is staggering testament to the ubiquity of the brand. There's also a circa 1930s soda fountain where an old-fashioned soda jerk will pour you a tall, cool one. Tours of the pavilion are self-guided; admission is on a first-come, first-served basis. Reservations are only made for groups of 25 or more. The World of Coke is one of the most popular tourists attractions in the city, so you can expect a wait to get in, especially during the summer. Allow two hours for the tour. You'll probably come away humming one of the old commercial jingles and feeling a vague sense of patriotism. It may be that only in America could an empire of this breadth, wealth and scope have been built upon a product that is—when you get down to it—nothing more than bubbly, flavored water. *Downtown*

The World of Coca-Cola Pavilion, 55 Martin Luther King, Jr. Drive; (404) 767-5151, Hours: Monday-Saturday 10:00 a.m. with last admission as 8:30 p.m., Sunday noon with last admission at 5:00 p.m. Admission: adults $3.50, seniors 55 and over $3, children 6-12 $2.50, children under 6 free with an adult.

27 / Dance, Dance, Dance

Dance Clubs

If you like to dance, you've come to the right city: Atlanta sports some of the hottest clubs in America. Unfortunately, like meteors, they tend to flame and crash. Two of the city's most sizzlin' dance halls, Berlin and The Vixen, recently closed. There's no indication the ones listed here will be turning off the lights anytime soon. Be advised: Call ahead. Also, check the weekly Leisure guide in the *Atlanta Journal/Constitution* for the most up-to-date information and hours. On weekends, the glitzier clubs generally don't start hopping until after midnight.

Velvet: Dark, gothic, exceedingly pretentious, Velvet—named by *Newsweek* magazine as one of the Top 10 dance clubs in America—cranks Disco/Techno music to the wee hours of the morning. The club features live acts. SoHo: Atlanta's Studio 54. Crowds line up at the door after midnight to be culled out by doormen who decide who's cool enough to pay $7 to get in. Music is high-decibel and disco. Backstreet: A nightlife fixture in the gay community, Backstreet has played the same high-energy disco every night for the past 15 years. Backstreet features regular female impersonator shows. Tongue & Groove: A Yupscale club catering to boomers, T&G plays dance music ranging from jazz to Hendrix to big band, changing nightly. Otto's: The most low-key of the group, Otto's appeals to an older, more elegant crowd who come to check out the singles scene and dance to soft rock and live jazz.

Velvet, 989 Park Place N.E.; (404) 681-9936. *Downtown*

SoHo, 187 Walton Street; (404) 222-0011. *Downtown*

Backstreet, 845 Peachtree Street N.E.; (404) 873-1986. *Midtown*

Tongue & Groove, 3055 Peachtreet Street N.E.; (404) 216-2325. *Buckhead*

Otto's, 265 East Paces Ferry Road; (404) 233-1133. *Buckhead*

28 / Gourmet Grits

City Grill

The City Grill is Atlanta's most stunningly opulent dining room. It's housed in one of the city's most picturesque and storied old office towers, the 18-story Hurt Building, which opened in 1913 and overlooks Woodruff Park in downtown, a block from Five Points. Diners come in through a 40-foot marble-walled rotunda crowned with an ornate, sunburst dome; walk up two curving flights of marbled stairs; and enter brass-and-glass door. Inside, polished black marble and custom carpet repeat the dome's color scheme in a massive 5,000-square foot room with gilt-topped columns, potted palms and a candelabra chandelier suspended from a 30-foot ceiling. A marble, oak-banistered stairway leads to balcony seating. The scene is backdropped with floor-to-ceiling murals and windows draped with gold curtains. Chef Roger Kaplan's food is every bit as spectacular as the setting: American with a strong Southern/Southwestern influence. House specialties: southern-fried quail (light, crisp, and juicy) with cream gravy and half-dollar sized pepper biscuits, split and served with raspberry-blackberry preserves ($8.50); non-breaded lump crabmeat crab cakes with chili-basil oils atop lemon linguine ($13.50); hickory-fried beef tenderloin with whipped potatoes, lacquered bacon (in brown sugar and molasses) and red-eye gravy ($12.50); barbecued shrimp on creamy grits ($13.00); seared crusted sea bass on a bed of Manhattan clam chowder with tortilla medallions and sautéed spinach. Save room for dessert: Pastry chef Mark Anstey makes a superb creme brulee. Coat and tie are a must at dinner; while lunch is more casual, a jacket is expected for men.

Downtown

City Grill, 50 Hurt Plaza; (404) 524-2489. Hours: lunch Monday-Friday 11:30 a.m.-2:30 p.m., dinner Sunday-Monday 5:30-11:00 p.m. Reservations recommended.

29 / Ted Turner's Excellent Adventure

CNN Center

From here Ted Turner conquers the globe. The center, originally a huge downtown mall sitting adjacent to the Omni sports and entertainment arena, is home to cable magnate Ted Turner's 24-hour Cable News Network (CNN). It's a six-block walk from the Five Points MARTA station and Underground Atlanta, which increasingly has become a corridor for walking tourists. Drop by the *Atlanta Journal/Constitution* to look at old framed front pages or wander next door to see the Monetary Museum (see separate listing) in the Federal Reserve building. One of the main draws of the center is the 45-minute guided CNN tour, which takes you behind the scenes of the network. You can gaze through glass partitions into the newsroom and watch anchors deliver breaking news. In the atrium of the center, the network airs a daily "Talk Back Live" program (1:00 p.m.). Tourists can watch from a railing above a circular, sunken studio and stages, or join the audience and ask questions on daily topics. Also on display are old MGM movie posters (Turner owns the MGM film library) and displays for Turner's regular series, *National Geographic Explorer* and *Jacques Cousteau*. There's also a model of the Oscar that MGM won for the Turner-owner classic, *Gone with the Wind*. Inside the atrium visit the Turner store, which sells logoed clothing from Turner channels and sports teams. The mall offers a variety of fast-food restaurants, a health club, Jocks & Jills sports bar, and Reggie's Pub, a British tavern and watering hole for Turner employees. There's a good chance you might see one or two CNN anchors stopping in for a refreshment.

Downtown

CNN Center, One CNN Center, corner of Marietta Street and Techwood Drive; (404) 827-2300. Hours: Saturday-Sunday 10:00 a.m.-4:00 p.m., Monday-Friday 10:00 a.m.-5:00 p.m. Admission: adults $5, seniors and children 6-12 $2.50, children under 5 free.

30 / Newest Downtown Planet

Planet Hollywood

Call this place the Planet of the Gapes: At lunch and dinner tourists will line up on the sidewalk just to get inside and ogle the scene. This is the stuff of make-believe and dreams: Vivien Leigh's *Gone with the Wind* green drapery hat, Sylvester Stallone's *Rambo* bowie knife, and Tom Hanks's football uniform from *Forrest Gump* all decorate the high-concept restaurant and bar owned by Arnold Schwarzenegger, Sylvester Stallone, Bruce Willis and wife Demi Moore. The Planet, which opened in spring of 1995 as the 24th restaurant in the chain, is the ersatz Hollywood glitz answer to Hard Rock cafe's ersatz rock 'n' roll glitz located across the street. Neither restaurant/bar is recommended for its food, but you really don't come to a place like this to eat anyway. If you're a tourist looking for a contact buzz—and an off-chance of actually seeing a big-time celebrity—the Planet is the place to be. Prepare to wait 30-45 minutes to get in, and during the Olympics the wait will likely last longer than the marathon. The Planet, like the Hard Rock, sells souvenirs and serves the standard bar food: hamburgers, pizza, chicken, salads, and sandwiches.

Downtown

Planet Hollywood, 218 Peachtree Street. N.W.; (404) 523-7300. Hours: 11:00-1:00 a.m. The bar stays open until 2:00 a.m.

31 / Restaurant with a Backbeat

Hard Rock Cafe

Touristy, long on glitz and short on sustenance, Atlanta's Hard Rock Cafe has the magnetic draw of a roadside reptile farm. People come here to check out the creatures (maybe a REAL rock star will put in an appearance), and gaze at the rock 'n' roll memorabilia that hangs from the walls. At lunch time and during peak tourist season, people will be lined up outside, waiting 30-45 minutes just to get in. The restaurant, a spectacular multitiered sprawl of dark wood, brass, glass, and pop icons will leave you agog. Each Hard Rock Cafe (the chain started in London in 1971 and has locations in seven countries and several U.S. cities) hews to a local theme, with splashes of genre collectibles. Here, a corner features items from the Macon, Ga.-based Allman Brothers Band, including guitars, a snare drum, and a blue jean jacket. Memorabilia from Madonna, Chubby Checker, Johnny Cash, Mick Jagger, Little Richard and numerous other rocking legends are scattered throughout the bar. The food is so-so (the chicken wings are a good bet), but you come here to graze on the scenery. Located across the street from Planet Hollywood, the newest entry into Atlanta's place-to-be-seen-place, the Hard Rock is worth the wait if you're a rock aficionado.

Downtown

Hard Rock Cafe, 215 Peachtree Street; (404) 688-7625. Hours: Monday-Sunday 11:00-2:00 a.m.

32 / Live If You Like It

Live Music

Unlike many larger cities (New York, Chicago, and New Orleans come to mind) where jazz is practically the native tongue—Atlanta has a difficult time keeping live jazz alive. In recent years, a funereal procession of clubs have opened and closed. Four of them, however, are bucking the odds of early death. They've been around a while now and are likely to still be in business when you read this. But call ahead.

Dante's Down the Hatch: Jazz nightly from 5:00 p.m.-1:00 a.m.; locations in Underground Atlanta and Buckhead. The Bar (Ritz-Carlton Atlanta): Jazz Thursday-Saturday night from 6:00 p.m.-1:00 a.m. The Bar (Ritz-Carlton Buckhead): Jazz Monday-Saturday nights 8:00 p.m.-midnight. La Carousel (Paschal's Hotel): Jazz Friday and Saturday nights 8:00 p.m.-2:00 a.m.

Rock and acoustic venues tend to come and go, too. Some of the steadier clubs include The Masquerade: Two-level concert venue, younger crowds, disco dance floor; Eddie's Attic: Acoustic music, mostly local bands; The Point: Avant-garde rock, mostly local in origin; Wreck Room: Cutting-edge local rock.

Dante's Down the Hatch, Underground Atlanta and 3380 Peachtree Rd. N.E.; (404) 266-1600 (both locations). *Buckhead*

The Bar (Ritz-Carlton Atlanta), 181 Peachtree St. N.E.; (404) 659-0400. *Downtown*

The Bar (Ritz-Carlton Buckhead), 3434 Peachtree Rd. N.E.; (404) 237-2700. *Buckhead*

La Carousel (Paschal's Hotel), 830 Martin Luther King Jr. Blvd.; (404) 577-3150. The Masquerade, 695 North Ave. N.E.; (404) 577-8178. *Downtown*

Eddie's Attic, 515-B N. McDonough St., Decatur, GA 30030; (404) 377-4976.

The Point, 420 Moreland Ave.; (404) 659-3522. *Little Five Points*

Wreck Room, 800 Marietta St. N.W.; (404) 874-8544. Call for covers and other information. *Downtown*

33 / Downtown and Top Notch

Marriott Marquis

The Marriott Marquis downtown hotel, with its curved glass exterior and 48-story atrium, is practically a tourist attraction unto itself. Designed by John Portman as the big brother to his Hyatt Regency Atlanta, the Marquis dominates the Peachtree Center skyline. Even those accustomed to open atrium hotels will gasp when they first enter the Marquis. The cavernous interior seems large and airy enough to require its own daily weather report. Massive sculptures cascade from the skylight and draping vines create a hanging garden effect. Bullet-shaped elevators swoop guests up to the hotel's 1,674 rooms and 80 suites. Sidewalk cafes, seafood restaurants, formal dining rooms and piano bars within the hotel offer practically every type of meal you could ask for. Facilities available include a swimming pool, health club, game room, drugstore, gift shop, florist and boutiques. There is 24-hour room service, valet parking, limousine service and an airport shuttle. A covered walkway connects the Marriott with the Peachtree Center shopping complex. A stay in the Marriott Marquis can be an adventure, but just a visit to the urban environment can leave you spellbound. Like the Buckhead Ritz, the Marquis is impeccably located within strolling distance of many downtown attractions and shopping. During the day, the vigorous visitor may want to walk from here to Underground Atlanta. It's a block west on Harris and about eight blocks south on Peachtree.

Downtown

Marriott Marquis, 265 Peachtree Center Ave.; (404) 521-0000.

34 / Where the Dream Lives On

Martin Luther King, Jr. Center for Nonviolent Social Change

This shrine, museum, and memorial to slain Civil Rights leader Reverend Martin Luther King, Jr., set in the neighborhood where he grew up, is one of Atlanta's top attractions and the preeminent African-American historic site in the country. Each year tens of thousands of national and international tourists and world leaders come here to pay homage to Dr. King's achievement and legacy: The passage of Civil Rights legislation in the 1960s, in large part the result of Dr. King's personal courage and sheer determination, was a giant step forward in the struggle for racial equality. The center, run by Dr. King's widow, Coretta Scott King, houses a library and archives with the world's largest collection of books and documents on the Civil Rights movement, including Dr. King's personal papers. The center also has a rare 87-volume edition of *The Collected Works of Mahatma Ghandi*, the assassinated Indian leader whose nonviolent methods of social change informed King's crusade for equality. The center is also the site of Dr. King's tomb, a marble crypt inscribed with his famous words, "Free at Last. Free at Last. Thank God Almighty, I'm Free at Last." Using a brochure as a map, visitors begin self-guided tours at the Exhibition Hall, which contains memorabilia of Dr. King's life and work: his Bible and preacher's robe; hand-written speeches and sermons; and the key to his room at the Lorraine Hotel in Memphis, where he was assassinated in 1968. In the Center's screening room, visitors can watch videos of King's historic "I Have a Dream" and "I've Been to the Mountaintop" speeches. The center holds an annual Kingfest during the summer, featuring live theatrical performances and music.

Downtown

Martin Luther King, Jr. Center for Nonviolent Social Change, 449 Auburn Ave.; (404) 524-1956. Hours: Sunday-Monday, 9:30 a.m.-5:30 p.m. Admission: Free. Videos: Children under 6 free; children 6-12 years old, 50¢; adults, $1.

35 / Stay Current on Currency

Monetary Museum at the Federal Reserve Bank of Atlanta

While the only thing you may know about money is that you don't have enough of it, a trip to the Monetary Museum will teach you all you will ever want to know about currency. The museum explains the evolution of currency throughout the world and the development of money and banking in the United States. On display are coins and currency including the rock money of Yap Island and the monetary policy of the people of the Kissi Tribe of Sierra Leone, Africa, who maintain if you peg seven pennies to the ground beside a man's door it will make a wife obey. Also exhibited are rare sets of coins, gold dust, gold nuggets and a 395.45-Troy-ounce gold bar that fluctuates in value based on the price of gold. (On the day the author visited, it was worth $148,520.) Also on display are sheets of uncut currency ranging from the $1.00 George Washington to $100,000 notes used only for transactions between the Federal Reserve and the Treasury (no, we're not going to tell you who is on it). There is also a video and a self-guided free tour that takes about 30 minutes. Tours for large groups can be arranged in advance. Remember that this is a Federal Reserve Bank and security is tight. You have to sign in and wear a visitor badge and no cameras are allowed in the building. Yes, they do give away souvenirs; unfortunately the money has been shredded. The Federal Reserve is located in downtown Atlanta and parking is available directly across the street.

Downtown

The Monetary Museum at the Federal Reserve Bank of Atlanta, 104 Marietta St.; (404) 521-8747. Hours: Monday-Friday, 9:00 a.m.-4:00 p.m. Closed on weekends and bank holidays.

36 / The Oldest Resting Place in Atlanta

Oakland Cemetery

Atlanta's Oakland Cemetery, an 88-acre tract on a hill 10 miles east of the city, is Atlanta's first graveyard and, figuratively at least, the soul of the city. Since its opening in 1850, Oakland has become the final resting place of more than 40,000 people from every walk of life, from paupers to some of Atlanta's most famous citizens. Those buried here include golfing legend Bobby Jones, *Gone With the Wind* author Margaret Mitchell, 2,500 Confederate soldiers, five Confederate generals, six governors of the state and 23 mayors of Atlanta (including the first one, Moses Formwalt). During the Battle of Atlanta, Confederate General J.B. Hood directed his troops from the second floor of a home on what is now the eastern portion of the cemetery. Two monuments to his troop's valor stand in the cemetery. Other reminders of Atlanta's varied history include segregated burial sites for Jews and African-Americans. Oakland also contains many stunning Victorian mausoleums and statues; in the early morning and late afternoon (the best time to visit), their long jagged shadows make a graveyard walk even eerier. A tour map in the Visitor's Center costs $1.25. From March to October there are regular guided tours on the weekend. Almost every grave has its own story and the guides can provide interesting insight into the lives of many of the residents. It's perfectly acceptable to bring a lunch and have a picnic at Oakland. Atlantans have been doing it for generations.

Downtown

Oakland Cemetery, 248 Oakland Ave; (404) 688-2107. Hours: The Visitor's Center is open Monday-Friday, 9:00 a.m.- 5:00 p.m. The cemetery is open seven days a week, 8:00 a.m.-7:00 p.m., during summer and 8:00 a.m.-6:00 p.m. in winter. Guided tours are offered March through October. Admission: adults, $3; children, $2.

37 / Interactive Science

SciTrek—The Science and Technology Museum of Atlanta

This is the place where really inquiring minds want to go. In fact, once inside you may wish you had listened to your eighth-grade science teacher. The 150 permanent interactive exhibits touch on virtually every aspect of physical science, from light and perception and electricity and magnetism to mathematics and machines. Kids and adults both can enjoy experimenting first hand with the underappreciated marvels of electricity, gravity, and, well, thin air. The center also features traveling displays, guest lectures, films, scientific demonstrations. SciTrek continues to grow and evolve: New exhibits are being added all the time. There are also occasions when SciTrek offers summer camps and overnight trips, so check with the museum to find out about upcoming events. The gift shop offers a wide range of science books and toys, as well as do-it-yourself home science projects. This is a popular stop for school groups during the school year so it can be crowded. Admission for groups of 12 or more can be arranged in advance and will offer a better rate than regular admission. Call SciTrek for details. If you have kids or wish you had been scientist, this is one stop not to miss. SciTrek is located next to the Atlanta Civic Center and ample parking is available, although it's a bit pricey at $4 a car. Allow at least two hours for your visit.

Downtown

SciTrek—The Science and Technology Museum of Atlanta, 395 Piedmont; (404) 522-5500. Hours: Monday-Saturday 10:00 a.m.-5:00 p.m.; Sunday noon-5:00 p.m. Admission: adults 18 and over $7.50; seniors, students and teachers with proper I.D. and children 3-17, $5.00; groups of 12 or more $4.50 if reservations are made two weeks in advance.

38 / Where the World Revolves Around You

The Sundial Room

One of the best and literally most moving views of Atlanta is from the Sundial Restaurant and Lounge atop the 73-story Westin Peachtree Plaza Hotel downtown, the tallest hotel in the United States. The two-story revolving restaurant on the 71st and 72nd floors of the hotel offers good food and a spectacular vista that guests don't have to move from their seats to appreciate. The bar revolves 360 degrees every hour. To get to the restaurant, ride glass elevators that run up the outside of the building; they are as thrilling as anything you'll find at Six Flags Over Georgia. If heights bother you, close your eyes. There is an observation floor you can visit just for the view, which costs, $1.00 per person. This fee is waived if you are having lunch or dinner. The food and service are good, but the prices in the Sundial match the neighborhood: They're sky-high (a 12-ounce filet mignon runs $34.95 for dinner). Dress is upscale casual. Reservations are strongly recommended for both lunch and dinner. During peak hours expect to wait. But, with the world revolving around you, you don't feel quite so neglected.

Downtown

The Sundial Room, 70th Floor, Westin Peachtree Plaza Hotel, 210 Peachtree St.; (404) 589-7506. Restaurant hours: lunch 11:30 a.m.-2:30 p.m., dinner Sunday-Thursday, 6:00-11:00 p.m., Friday and Saturday 6:00-11:30 p.m. Sunday brunch served 10:30 a.m.-2:30 p.m.

Lounge Hours: Monday-Friday 2:00 p.m.-1:45 a.m.; Saturday 11:30-1:45 a.m.; Sunday 12:30 p.m.-12:45 a.m.

39 / A Soulful Restaurant
Thelma's Kitchen

The traveler's search for soul food can take him or her to many venues in Atlanta, but he or she can save shoe leather by dropping in at Thelma's Kitchen. The stark, 1940s-style cafeteria off the downtown business district offers the most soulful, rib-sticking, modestly priced ($3-$7) victuals in town. For years Thelma's has been a popular breakfast stop for downtown workers not particularly worried about arterial sclerosis. The restaurant serves a hearty breakfast with the usual trappings: eggs made to order, grits (done right), superb biscuits, and sides of bacon and sausage, or excellent salmon cakes. The restaurant's main draw, however, is lunch, when patrons line up at steam tables to select from an assortment of Deep South favorites: excellent fried chicken (crisp and moist); macaroni and cheese; okra pancakes; country-fried steak; barbecued chicken; baked ham; and an assortment of vegetables including squash, lima beans, green beans, okra, scalloped potatoes, candied yams, rice and gravy and collard greens. The restaurant is family run by Thelma and Riley Grundy and has a devoted downtown clientele who jam the place during lunch on weekdays. Regulars include CNN personnel (CNN Center is a few blocks south) and Atlanta sports figures (Braves all-star outfielder David Justice is a devotee, as well as former heavyweight boxing champ Evander Holyfield). Thelma's serves lunch late, but no dinner. Either come before 11:30 a.m. or after 1:00 p.m. to avoid a wait. *Be advised:* Thelma's may be forced to relocate as a result of Olympic construction, so call first.

Downtown

Thelma's Kitchen, 190 Luckie Street; (404) 688-5885. Hours: Monday-Friday 7:30 a.m.-5:00 p.m. Take out is available.

40 / Shopping Below the Surface

Underground Atlanta

New Orleans has the French Quarter, San Francisco the Wharf. Atlanta has Underground Atlanta as its central tourist lure. In its original incarnation in the 1960s and early '70s, the district had about it a certain gaslit, wild-west appeal. The new version, domesticated by a Rouse Company revamping, while offering glimpses of the city's past, is mainly a shopping mall. Underground's origin dates to the 1920s when the city built viaducts over railroad tracks in the center of town. For years the area was abandoned. A group of enterprising businesspeople reopened the street as Underground Atlanta in 1969, envisioning it as an entertainment district with bars, shops and restaurants. In the early years it boomed, then died, the victim of downtown crime, City Hall's indifference and MARTA construction. In the late 1980s, the city—realizing the defunct district still retained its marquee appeal to visitors who constantly asked about it—enlisted Rouse (developer of Baltimore's Harborplace and New York's South Street Seaport) and, with a $142 million investment, Underground was refurbished and reopened in 1989. The complex continues to lose about $2 million a year. Visitors should start the day early, no better place than Café du Mond, with a cup of chicory-laced café au lait and a round of powder-sugar-dusted beignets. Pick up a map of the complex at the Visitor's Center on Upper Alabama Street and stroll around. Underground hosts more than 100 shops, restaurants, bars and night spots. Live music in Kenny's Alley is the main attraction at night. *A word of caution:* Underground is well-patrolled by police, but at night it's better to take a cab or MARTA back to your hotel. A covered corridor takes you directly from Underground to MARTA's Five Points Station.

Downtown

Underground Atlanta, between Peachtree St. and Central Ave.; (404) 577-2148. Hours: Monday-Saturday 10:00 a.m.-9:30 p.m., Sunday noon-6:00 p.m. Most restaurants and clubs stay open past midnight.

41 / World's Largest Drive-in Restaurant

The Varsity

A trip to Atlanta should not be considered complete without a stop at The Varsity. This Atlanta institution is not for the vegetarian or health-food addict. It's for the people who eat hot dogs and doesn't ask what's in them but, rather, what's ON them? Here, they've found the promised land. The Varsity has been serving hamburgers, onion rings, French fries and hot dogs to Atlantans for more than 60 years and brought the chili dog to an art form. A couple of dogs, an order of rings accompanied by a Jumbo F.O. (a large frozen orange drink that will actually lower your body temperature) and you're as close to nirvana as you can get at the to-go window. The food is made fresh and The Varsity taste is unique. Once you have tasted one and have a craving for another nothing else in the world will satisfy you. The Varsity is the largest drive-in restaurant in the world and still offers curb service. Some of the carhops have worked there for years and the way they move through a crowded lunchtime can be entertainment in itself. If you want to go inside, there is ample free parking. You place your order at a long counter behind which is an assembly line of fast food. Even at the busiest times it usually only takes a few minutes to get your meal. The interior of The Varsity is generally clean and neat with primary seating at Formica tables in large windowed rooms. The Varsity is across the street from the Georgia Tech campus; during football season, when Tech has a home game, it is a crowded tradition.

Downtown

The Varsity, 61 North Ave.; (404) 881-1706. Hours: Sunday-Thursday 9:00 a.m.-11:30 p.m., Friday and Saturday 9:00 a.m.-2:00 a.m.

42 / A Good Place to See Someone
Adult Entertainment

Atlanta may present itself as the next great international city, but it is still smack in the middle of the Bible Belt. In Atlanta, you can not rent X-rated films. Nevertheless, Atlanta has a healthy adult entertainment marketplace with first-rate clubs scattered across the metropolitan area. Don't go cruising for flashy neon signs or huge billboards with pictures of "nekkid women." The signs will let you know they are adult entertainment establishments, but from the outside, they look like regular bars. This type of entertainment is not for everyone, so if it offends you, avoid it. If it does not, the three listed here are among the best in Atlanta. All three offer real food (not just bar snacks), valet parking—and are closed on Sunday.

The Gold Club: Located on the north side of downtown, this is the Rolls-Royce of adult clubs in Atlanta. Entertainment is offered on four stages in a cavernous room lit by strobes and colored lights. Skits and Las Vegas-style "revues" are the featured entertainment. The Goldrush Showbar: Conventioneers often make this south side club their last stop on the way to the airport. The specialty here is entertainment by national artists: strippers, porno stars, centerfolds and Miss Nude World contestants. The Goldrush seems to take itself less seriously than other places and has a more "good ol' boy" atmosphere. The Cheetah Lounge: This club has been bachelor-party central in Atlanta for years. It's in downtown, a short drive or cab ride from most of the major hotels.

The Gold Club, 2416 Piedmont Road; (404) 233-1210. Dinner and a wee-hours breakfast buffet served. Call for hours and admission rates.

The Goldrush Showbar, 2608 Stewart Avenue; (404) 766-2532. Lunch and dinner are served. Call for hours and rates.

The Cheetah Lounge, 887 Spring Street; (404) 893-3037. A full menu of lunch and dinner selections is available. Call for hours and rates.

43 / The In-Town Neighborhood
Midtown

Atlanta's most artful, gay, urban and urbane neighborhood, Midtown reminds one of New York's SoHo district, not in the way it looks—there are yards, shady streets, and houses instead of high-rises, lofts and sidewalk flats—but in the way the neighborhood feels. If you're an Atlanta artist you probably live here or in Little Five Points. There are sections of the district that are still seedy. The neighborhood fell into decay during the '60s and '70s. Renovation efforts have brought much of Midtown back, with a number of outstanding Victorian homes in full splendor. Although at night that are sections where it is not safe to walk alone unless your name is Rottweiler, on sunny days during the weekend there's no better intown neighborhood to prowl. Start at the intersection of 10th Street and Peachtree. Notable spots include Frijoles, a cool, punk Mexican restaurant with streetside seating; and Da Pulcinella, which serves imaginative (and low-priced) Italian in atmospheric surroundings. Down the street are two other superb choices, the Touch of India Tandoori & Curry Restaurant, and Cha-Gio Vietnamese Restaurant. (See our separate listing for the wonderful French Quarter Food Shop Restaurant on the same stretch of Peachtree Street.) If you'd like to skate through midtown, Skate Escape is the place to rent in-lines; it's across the street from Piedmont Park.

Frijoles, 1031 Peachtree St. N.E.; (404) 892-8226.

Da Pulcinella, 1027 Peachtree St. N.E.; (404) 892-6195.

Touch of India Tandoori & Curry Restaurant, 962 Peachtree St. N.E.; (404) 876-7777.

Cha-Gio Vietnamese Restaurant, 966 Peachtree St. N.E.; (404) 855-9387.

44 / A Trip to Santa Fe
Sundown Cafe

The Sundown Cafe is a trip to Sante Fe without the airfare. The decor doesn't need to strain for authenticity—there are chili charts, Southwestern art and enough cactus to know you're probably not in Delaware—and the food is topnotch. Like many Atlanta restaurants, the Sundown doesn't accept reservations; most nights there's a wait. Use that as an excuse to have a margarita at the bar. Then take your table and eagerly await the chips and salsa while you peruse the menu, which has one foot in Mexico and the other north of the border. Crack the big blue and yellow corn tortilla chips into pieces and dip away. Sundown offers 15 varieties of salsa from green table (piquant and nutty) to salsa picosa (hot enough to burn the lips off a pair of vise grips). All are transcendent. Center cards in the menu announce extensive specials. They're foolproof (especially the seasoned ranchero steak, tender and tasty enough to cause sleepless nights). The side of spicy turnip greens with onions and chunks of tomato puts the domestic variety to shame. Other highlights include Enchiladas Espinaquas (two white corn tortillas stuffed with sautéed fresh spinach and topped with baby Chihuahua cheese and green New Mexico chili sauce); Pescado Sundown (a filet of tilapia dipped in Creole mustard egg wash, rolled in blue corn meal, fried and topped with pablaño tartar sauce); and Eddie's Pork (medallions of charbroiled pork loin with sides of tangy tequila barbecue sauce and roasted jalapeño gravy for dipping). Recommended dessert: the chocolate chimichanga with tequila sauce.

Midtown

Sundown Cafe, 2165 Cheshire Bridge Rd.; (404) 321-1118. Hours: lunch, Wednesday-Friday 11:00 a.m.-2:00 p.m.; dinner, Monday-Thursday 5:30-10:00 p.m.; Friday and Saturday 5:30-11:00 p.m.

45 / Midtown Sports Joint

The Beer Mug

If there were ever a place more appropriately named than The Beer Mug, you would be hard pressed to find it. This is one of the oldest sports bars in Atlanta and it has the feel of a big, friendly beer hall. The Beer Mug is really one large room with a serving bar in the middle. On one side of the bar tables are crowded together and you can watch your favorite sporting event on a big-screen television. On the other side of the room you can usually find a game of darts or pool in progress. The Beer Mug sits right on Peachtree Street, and there are outside tables when the weather co-operates, making it a great place to sit out in the evening. The food is above-average bar fare and you can get a little bit of everything, including pretty good pizza for a nonpizza place. Prices are reasonable and a variety of beers is offered by the bottle, mug, or pitcher. The service is generally good, and this is a place accustomed to dealing with large groups. It is not unusual to see local softball, rugby or flag football teams huddled in a corner celebrating their victory or nursing their wounds. Many weekend ballplayers have sat in the The Beer Mug in front of a slice of pizza and a cold beer and wondered why they couldn't go from first to third on a single to right field, knowing full well the answer, in part, is sitting in front of them. The Beer Mug draws a good crowd, especially on weekends, so there are times when tables are in short supply. Parking is free but can be scarce on the weekends in the evening. This is a great place to have a cold beer and talk about the things you use to do.

Midtown

The Beer Mug, 1705 Peachtree Street; (404) 874-7836. Hours: Monday-Friday 11:00 a.m.-2:00 a.m., Saturday noon-3:00 a.m., Sunday noon-2:00 a.m.

46 / Movies the Way They Were Meant to Be Seen

Fox Theater

Some people are still miffed at Ma Bell for trying to tear down this architectural wonder in the early 1970s to erect the nondescript office tower that now looms next door. Fortunately, public opinion and a grassroots "Save the Fox" campaign saved the 1920s movie palace. The Fox, which occupies most of a block at the intersection of Peachtree Street and Ponce de Leon Avenue, is by far the most architecturally significant and acoustically sound performance hall in the South. Influenced by American's Egyptian craze in the 1920s (some of the art and furnishings are replicas from the tomb of King Tut), the architecture is an exotic blend of Egyptian, Moorish and Turkish motifs, featuring minarets and onion domes on the outside and a faux star-lit Arabian courtyard as the main hall inside. Over the years, some of America's greatest performers have played here, and for two decades the Metropolitan Opera performed in the Fox for a week each summer. Since its restoration, performers have ranged from Bruce Springstein to Liza Minnelli to Jerry Seinfeld. Fox tours led by Bob Van Camp (who actually lives in the building) take you through the history of the theater and conclude with Van Camp's demonstration of the 3,600-pipe Moller organ, one of the largest in the world. The Fox is one of the few aspects of Atlanta history that hasn't been effaced by the city's rush to redefine itself architecturally as the New South. A chance to see any kind of performance here should not be missed; otherwise, the tour is well worth your time.

Midtown

Fox Theater, 660 Peachtree Street N.E.; (404) 881-1977. Hours: tours on Monday and Thursday, 10:00 a.m.; Saturday at 10:00 and 11:30 a.m. Admission: tours $5 for adults, $3 for students and seniors.

47 / Atlanta Center for the Arts

High Museum of Art

Atlanta's artistic renaissance can be dated from 1983, the year the city opened the High Museum's new building on Peachtree Street adjacent to the Woodruff Arts Center. The new museum finally provided the appropriate setting for the art collections begun by the High in 1926. The $20-million white porcelain and glass building, designed by New York architect Richard Meier, is itself a work of art and one of the few architecturally redeeming structures erected during the city's three-decade building boom. Inside, four floors of galleries are separated by semicircular ramps that curve around a four-story sun-splashed atrium. As Atlanta's largest museum, the High's permanent collection includes works by Monet, O'Keeffe and Rodin; 19th- and 20th-century American painters; and Hudson River school artists Thomas Cole, Frederic Church, Thomas Sully, John Singer Sargent and William Harnett. European artists on display in the third-floor gallery include Giovanni Bellini, Jan Breughel the Elder, and Giovanni Battasta Tiepolo. The second floor houses the Virginia Carroll Crawford collection of English Ceramics, featuring place settings commissioned by 18th- and 19th-century nobility and the Richman Collection of African art. A fourth-floor display, "Early Modernism: The Roots of Abstractionism," features pieces by Gorky, Soutine and others. The "Poetic Gesture" exhibit on the fourth-floor included Abstract Impressionist works by such artists as Frankenthaler, Gottlieb, Rothko and Gilliam. The High regularly hosts major traveling exhibits as well as regular lectures, workshops, and multi media exhibits.

Midtown

High Museum of Art, 1280 Peachtree Street N.E.; (404) 733-4200. Hours: Sunday noon-5:00 p.m.; Tuesday, Wednesday, Thursday and Saturday 10:00 a.m.-5:00 p.m.; Friday 10:00 a.m.-9:00 p.m., closed Monday. Admission: adults $4, senior citizens and students with I.D. $2, children 6-17 $1, children under 6 free. Free for all on Thursdays, 1:00-5 p.m.

48 / Indoor Mardi Gras
French Quarter Food Shop

It's certified hole in the wall (with sidewalk seating under a canopy) that reeks of Mardi Gras and serves the most authentic Cajun food in the city. Small, totally unpretentious (next door to one of the city's finest certified dives, the Stein Club), the French Quarter sports black-and-white tiled floors and dingy walls decorated in French Quarter art and Mardi Gras beads. Most nights the place bustles with a mixed-Midtown crowd that ranges from businesspeople to yuppies to gays to the occasional drag queen. Cramped seating and insistent clamor from the kitchen only heighten the impression that this place clearly puts food above atmosphere. Every dish, from po' boys to skillet-prepared soft-shell crab is superb and served in healthy plate-filling portions. The gumbo is rich, spicy and full of andouille sausage. Better crawfish étouffé and shrimp jambalya can't be found anywhere north of New Orleans. Red beans and rice cooked in a stock of ham hocks and andouille is spicy and unforgettable. Hands down, the French Quarter serves the best fried oysters in town, lightly battered, juicy, crisp and peppery, served with a choice of two rich remoulade sauces. The restaurant also serves a grilled muffaletta sandwich of salami and provolone, topped with a relish of black olives, mushrooms and artichoke hearts. The French Quarter offers a small selection of wines and beers, including the lethal Blackened Voodoo. Save something for desert. House specialty is a bread pudding spiced with cinnamon and smothered in a bourbon-laced butter sauce that will haunt you for weeks. *One note:* At this writing, plans are to expand the restaurant; we only hope that's the only change.

Midtown

French Quarter Food Shop, 923 Peachtree Street; (404) 875-2489. Hours: Lunch Monday-Friday 11:00 a.m.-2:00 p.m., Saturday 11:30 a.m.-2:30 p.m., Dinner Tuesday-Saturday 6:00-10:00 p.m. No reservations.

49 / 24-Hour Nights
Club Anytime

This is the place your mother warned you about. Club Anytime is big and barny and open 24 hours a day. If you just have to have that bourbon at 8:27 a.m., this is the place. During the early evening hours, the club is sedate and almost deserted. But after midnight, all manner of creatures great and small migrate to Club Anytime. Straights, gays, reprobates, would-be reprobates, wanna-be reprobates, nightcrawlers and daydreamers will all be lined up waiting to get in. To avoid the crowd, arrive before 2:00 a.m. By 3:00 a.m. there will be a line outside and wall-to-wall people inside. Because Club Anytime is open 24 hours, this is the place where bartenders, dancers, bouncers and all your basic late-night service industry people go to relax when their establishments close. Between 3:00 and 5:00 a.m. the DJ will be spinning the music and the place will be jammed and jamming. Burgers and sandwiches are available. There are also pool tables, table soccer and video games, but the spotlight is on the huge dance floor. When the shank of the evening arrives, the party is just starting. If you are a late-night person—or just want to take a walk (or crawl) on the wild side—then fit Club Anytime in on your schedule at 4:00 a.m.

Midtown

Club Anytime, 1055 Peachtree Street; (404) 607-8050. Open 24 hours, seven days a week.

50 / Blues and Bar-B-Q

Fat Matt's Rib Shack

Port meets the blues; it's an art movement you can eat, with cold beer on the side. Can you think of a better way to spend a Saturday night? All Fat Matt's lacks is a dance floor, a small sacrifice for the cramped club in Midtown where regulars jam the place on weekends for finger-licking barbecue (pork sandwiches, ribs, Brunswick stew—the usual) and hot blues performed by local bands. Decor is as spare as the seating space at small tables in this converted strip retail store. The back wall behind the tiny bandstand features a mural of blues legends Robert Johnson, Muddy Waters, Willie Dixon and Bobby Blair. There's also seating in booths on an outside patio where the band is in clear view. There's never any trouble hearing the music, which is deafening. Often guitarists with wireless jacks will wander the room and the deck while performing riffs. Come early if you just want barbecue, buy it at the counter (no credit cards) and pick a table. (Outside smoking only.) The music cranks up at 10:00 p.m. Regular performers include local acts such as Frankie Lee Robinson and the Solid Senders, Southside Jukes, Fistful of Chitlins, Rough Draft, Mickey's Big Mouth Jam and Chicken Shack. Fat Matt's also has periodic open-mike nights and an occasional blues star (Jimmy Rodgers, Jr.) will drop in. On weekends, crowds line up at the door.

Midtown

Fat Matt's Rib Shack, 1811 Piedmont Road N.E.; (404) 607-1622. Hours: Monday-Thursday 11:30 a.m.-11:30 p.m., Friday and Saturday 11:30-1:00 a.m.

51 / Southern Cooking Home Style

Colonnade Restaurant

A visit to Atlanta without southern fried chicken is like a trip to Kansas City without a T-bone. And though there are many pretenders and aspirants to the title, the Colonnade makes the best fried chicken in town. But it didn't get to be an Atlanta institution with fried chicken alone. A nondescript, ranch-style building along the spicy/seedy strip of shops, bars and restaurants on Cheshire Bridge Road between Midtown and Buckhead, the restaurant has a no-style style, but it's been packing in a loyal clientele since 1972; regulars include an increasingly hip Midtown crowd and a few of those rarities, the Atlanta native. Come early and have a drink in the bar next to the fireplace while waiting for your table. Some nights, the wait can be 30 minutes or more. Eventually, you'll be seated in the sprawling main dining room (butcher block tables and English print art) and order from big-haired waitresses who've been here for eons. Fried chicken's a must, but there are plenty of can't-fail options: braised lamb shank; sugar-cured ham in redeye gravy; country fried steak; frilled rainbow trout; salmon croquettes with egg sauce and fried chicken livers. All come with a choice of vegetables—including homemade whipped potatoes, exquisite sweet potato soufflé, macaroni and cheese, black-eyed peas, collard greens, stewed okra and tomatoes—and with homemade cornbread and melt-in-your-mouth yeast rolls. Portions are huge. But save room for dessert. Favorites: the hot fudge cake, apple pie á la mode, and brandy peach ice cream.

Midtown

Colonnade Restaurant, 1879 Cheshire Bridge Road N.E.; (404) 874-5642. Hours: lunch Monday-Saturday 11:00 a.m.-2:30 p.m., dinner Monday-Saturday 5:00 p.m.-9:00 p.m., Sunday 11:00 a.m.-8:30 p.m. No reservations.

52 / The Home of Atlanta's Favorite Crab Cakes

Chef's Cafe

Half a block down Piedmont Avenue from the Tattletale strip lounge, this San Francisco-style bistro has its own tale to tell: It's one of Atlanta's hidden culinary delights. Tucked humbly away in the quarters of a Comfort Inn, between the sybaritic haunts of Midtown and Buckhead, this cozy, casually elegant restaurant with crab cakes to die for (the city's best) belies the lowered expectations of its setting. Chef Justin Ward's innovative menu varies from season to season, leans heavily to seafood and chicken, and is spectacularly executed from appetizer to desserts. All fish are fresh, the restaurant bakes its own bread, and greens are grown to specification by local farmers. Lit a little too bright to be termed romantic, tables for two are tiny enough to invite their own intimacy. Service is brisk and friendly. The restaurant offers a select list of 35 (mostly California) wines. Most entrées come in appetizer portions, so there's no excuse for not indulging the crab cakes with a spicy remoulade (and a side of jalapeño tartar sauce), the best this writer has eaten on any coast. For an entrée, try the fettuccine and grilled chicken (with sun-dried tomatoes, julienne eggplant in olive oil, mixed herbs and goat cheese), or sautéed rainbow trout with shallots, wine grape sauce, wild mushrooms, and a side of mashed potatoes. Vegetarians will salivate over the marinated and grilled vegetable plate laced with a sun-dried tomato infused oil. The Chef's Cafe also serves what many think is the best Sunday brunch in town. Brunch prices range from $5 to $10.95. At dinner, prices start at $5.95 for appetizers and range between $7.95 and $18.50 for entrées.

Midtown

Chef's Cafe, 2115 Piedmont Rd.; (404) 872-2284. Hours: dinner Sunday-Thursday 6:00-10:00 p.m., Friday-Saturday 6:00-11:00 p.m.; Sunday Brunch 11:00 a.m.-2:30 p.m. Reservations recommended.

53 / Print in Its Prime

The Old New York Book Shop

At first glance, The Old New York Book Shop looks forgettable, almost regrettable. But, once past the run-down exterior, the book lover will find a gold mine of hard-to-find old volumes. The owner, Cliff Graubart, has been selling books from this same old house since 1974 and he's a demon for quality; this is not a knickknack store or flea market. Over 20,000 volumes, mostly hardbacks, line the shelves, and wandering the halls give you the feeling you might have stumbled into *Citizen Kane*'s private library. The majority of the offerings come from private collections and are in quite good condition. The coffee-stained, bent-spine, dog-eared book is seldom seen. Prices run anywhere from $5 to $5,000 for rare prints or editions, but you can add some high-toned titles to your home library for less than $20. Books are shelved according to subject matter and employees can point you to the right place if you simply must have a biography of Hart Crane. The Old New York Book Shop has hosted a number of autograph parties and book signings, and its scuffed well-worn floors are considered hallowed ground for many Atlanta writers. It is one block off Peachtree Street; if you are one of those people who just love books, plan to kill a couple of hours here.

Midtown

The Old New York Book Shop, 1069 Juniper St.; (404) 881-1285. Hours: Tuesday-Friday, 11:00 a.m.-6:00 p.m., Saturday, 10:00 a.m.-6:00 p.m. Closed Sunday and Monday.

54 / Central Park Southern Style

Piedmont Park

Designed by the fella who laid out Central Park, Frederick Law Olmsted, 185-acre Piedmont Park is as elemental to the sanity of Atlanta as Central Park is to New York City. On weekends the rolling hills, vast green fields and woodlands of the sprawling park are a hive of urban apartment fever uncorked: bicyclists, skaters, joggers, kids, parents with children in strollers, street musicians, and sunbathers abound. The park is a perfect starting point for a walking tour of Atlanta's best intown neighborhoods. It's bordered on the west by Ansley Park (the city's most picturesque neighborhood), on the south by Midtown, and on the east by Virginia-Highlands. Piedmont was the site of the seminal 1895 Cotton States Exhibition which—along with Sherman and Coca-Cola—put Atlanta on the national map. The event was attended by luminaries including President Grover Cleveland and John Philip Sousa, who composed the "King Cotton March" for the occasion. In recent years, the park has been the site of innumerable musical events, including concerts by the Allman Brothers, Elton John, the Atlanta Jazz Festival, and a series of summer performances by the Atlanta Symphony. The park hosts the annual Dogwood Festival in the spring, the Atlanta Arts Festival in the fall, and is the finishing line for the annual July 4th Peachtree Road Race. Among Piedmont's features are a 3-mile jogging trail, a duck pond, a playground with jungle gyms, 13 tennis courts and 2 softball fields. The park is adjacent to a number of bars and restaurants within easy walking distance. Like most urban parks, Piedmont is not safe after dark.

Midtown

Piedmont Park, 14th Street and Piedmont Avenue; (404) 658-7406. Hours: 6:00 a.m.-11:00 p.m.

55 / Where Strings Are Attached

Center For Puppetry Arts

Before MTV, before Nintendo—for that matter, before Marconi—
when child's play was simple, the puppet and the marionette
provided the magic. A place to rekindle that magic is the Atlanta
Center for Puppetry Arts. If you have children, make it a high
priority for your Atlanta visit, although adults will find it just as
delightful. The Center features the world's largest private
collection of puppets and marionettes, ranging from showbizzy
Muppets (an original is on display) to ritualistic African figures to
ancient artifacts (clay puppets used 700 years ago in religious
ceremonies by South American Indians). But a puppet without a
performance is just a doll. The Center brings its puppets to life
with full-scale productions that feature elaborate sets and costumes
and a setting—an intimate 300-seat auditorium—inviting the
audience to another place, another time. Christmas is the Center's
high season, when children really get a kick out of holiday-themed
productions of classic Yuletide stories such as "Rudolph the Red-
Nosed Reindeer." Year-round the center stages productions of
familiar stories: "Pinocchio," "Cinderella," "Beauty and the Beast."
Traveling puppetry companies often bring more adult-oriented
evening plays to town ("Voice of the Hollow Man"). In addition
to the main auditorium, the Center has three smaller theaters, a
gift shop, reference library and educational facilities. In the
Puppetworks display area children are invited to operate puppets
and marionettes themselves.

Midtown

Center for Puppetry Arts, 1404 Spring St.; (404) 873-3391. Call box
office for hours. Admission: Performances $5.50; Museum $3 for adults,
$2 for children, complimentary for those attending a show or workshop.

56 / Good Place to Find a Gertrude Stein

The Stein Club

You thought this place was named after the cold beer sold here. Nope. This semi-squalid dive fronting Peachtree Street (next door to the splendid French Quarter Food Shop) is named after Lost Generation writer Gertrude Stein—and lost generations have been coming here for the last 25 years. If Dylan Thomas were somehow laid over—and hung over—in Atlanta, you get the feeling you would have found him here. The Stein Club is the city's closest thing to New York's White Horse Tavern. It's not the place to eat, though bar food is served. It's the atmosphere that's delectable. The haunt of pained writers and mentally blocked sculptors (the founder is a sculptor), the cerebral come here to be the "scene" and heard. During the Stein Club's annual Bloomsday celebration (June 16), reading from James Joyce's *Ulysses* while standing atop a table (and falling under one has been known to happen) is considered de rigueur. The bar's annual Atlanta Open Orthographic Meet is a chance for denizens to show they can spell the polysyllabics they've been tossing around over chess matches for the past 12 months. Pop by to catch the game on TV or dance to one of Atlanta's best and most schizophrenic juke boxes. One quarter will get you the Country classic, "Born to Lose"; another will buy you Bunny Berigan's "I Can't Get Started." If a night on the town is what you have in mind, you won't have any trouble getting started here, a place where one beer, for some reason, feels like a six-pack anywhere else.

Midtown

The Stein Club, 929Peachtree St., N.E.; (404) 876-3707. Hours: Saturday and Sunday 6:00 p.m.-3:00 a.m., Monday 3:00 p.m.-4:00 a.m., Tuesday-Thursday, 3:00 p.m.-3:00 a.m.

57 / The City's Best Burger

The Vortex Bar & Grill

Downtown workers in search of an after-office pop can be found in The Vortex, a smoky, comfortably cramped two-story bar at the foot of 11th and West Peachtree in Midtown. But there's more to this bar than one of the biggest selections of imported (45) and domestic (60) beers in the city, a staggering array of shooters (from Kamikazes to the more esoteric Mind Eraser), and mixed drinks. The Vortex is famous for its hamburgers, which we'll go ahead and concede are the best in town. Made of eight ounces of ground sirloin, grilled to perfection, and served on a toasted sesame seed bun with a side of light, crispy fries or potato salad, they're juicy, every so slightly smoky, and mouthwateringly delicious. The quarter-pound pure beef Big Fat Vortex Dog is equally savory. Decor-wise, the Vortex resembles a flea market turned upside down. Walls are decorated with posters, hub caps, and old advertisements. A veritable junk yard of restored gimcracks dangle from the ceiling. After work, the crowd tends to yuppies and media types; later on, the crowd tends to get louder and more heavily weighted with bikers and singles on the prowl. But the owners—siblings Hank, Michael and Suzanne Benoit—keep things in check with a style that's tongue-in-cheek. "We reserve the right to refuse service to anyone, especially if we think that you're a great big jerk," reads the restaurant's "Idiot" policy on the back of the menu. In our experience, the service was brisk, but The Vortex comes with a guarantee that pretty well sums up the place: "If you are not serviced within five minutes, then you'll be served within ten or fifteen. Don't get a knot in your shorts, just relax and enjoy the atmosphere."

Midtown

The Vortex Bar & Grill, 1041 West Peachtree Street N.E.; (404) 875-1667. Hours: Monday-Friday 11:30-2:00 a.m., Saturday and Sunday 6:00 p.m.-2:00 a.m.

58 / Not Just Your Typical Southern Breakfast

Bagels

As recently as 25 years ago, the bagel was a curiosity in the South, rare as grits in Boston. With the expansion of Atlanta's population and the influx of Northerners with predilections for lox, the bagel has become as ubiquitous in Atlanta as sweet iced tea. They're sold in grocery stores, donut shops and even on some golf courses. Atlanta hosts a number of first-rate deli/bagel shops, notable among them The Royal Bagel in Midtown and Goldberg's in Buckhead. The Royal Bagel in Midtown feels more like a bake shop, but it offers the usual toppings (lox, nova, whitefish) and fresh bagels baked on the premises. The crowds tend to be trendy but then, so does the neighborhood. Goldberg's, a Buckhead fixture for 22 years—stuck obscurely in a storefront in a strip shopping center on Roswell Road—feels more like New York. On Sunday mornings in warm weather, couples sit at sidewalk tables with bagels, coffee, and *The New York Times*. Goldberg's bagels, like the Royal Bagel's, are baked on the premises and are often served still warm. Goldberg's also serves sandwiches (including brisket pastrami, hot Romanian pastrami, and kosher hot dogs). The restaurant sells breads by the loaf and has a wide variety of beverages, from Coke to Cel-Ray, in its cold box.

Royal Bagel, 1544 Piedmont Ave N.E.; (404) 876-3512. Hours: Monday-Saturday, 7:00 a.m.-5:00 p.m.; Sunday 7:00-4:00 p.m. *Midtown*

Goldberg's, 4383 Roswell Rd. N.E.; (404) 256-3751. Hours: opens daily at 7:00 a.m.; Monday until 3:00 p.m., Tuesday-Thursday until 5:00 p.m., Friday until 6:00 p.m., Saturday until 5:00 p.m., Sunday until 4:00 p.m. *Buckhead*

59 / Places to Go to See People Putting on an Act

Theater

Atlanta was once a live-theater wasteland, but no more. These days, Atlanta stages showcase everything from traditional to off-the-wall theatrical productions. Check weekly guides to see what's on while you're in town, and always phone ahead to check ticket availability. Here are a few best choices:

Alliance Theater: This is generally regarded the "establishment" theater in Atlanta. Located in the Woodruff Arts Center, Alliance stages quality mainstream works; productions have included "A Streetcar Named Desire" and "Much Ado About Nothing." On Stage Atlanta: Performances are usually crisp and well rehearsed at this theater, whose varied offerings have included "The Little Shop of Horrors" and "The Glass Menagerie." Horizon Theater: This group produces quality contemporary works such as "The Heidi Chronicles" and "Escape from Happiness." Seven Stages: Here you'll find new or little-known works that push the boundaries of traditional theater—and usually provide an interesting evening. Seven Stages has become a proving ground for fledgling playwrights. Agatha's—A Taste of Mystery: This dinner theater with a "whodunit" twist can be a fun evening when you're in the mood. The five-course dinners are good, but the fun begins as patrons are given roles in the evening's play. We know—the waiter did it!

Alliance Theater, 1280 Peachtree Street; (404) 892-2414. *Midtown*

On Stage Atlanta, 420 Courtland St.; (404) 897-1802. *Downtown*

Horizon Theater, 1083 Austin Ave.; (404) 584-7450. *Little Five Points*

Seven Stages, 1105 Euclid Ave.; (404) 523-7647. *Little Five Points*

Agatha's—A Taste of Mystery, 693 Peachtree St.; (404) 875-1610. *Downtown*

60 / In-Town Shopping and Entertainment

Virginia-Highlands

Nobody has proposed enclosing Virginia-Highlands in a mall, but its seems the logical next step in this once quiet, blue-collar, college-kid-in-rental-property neighborhood that has gone totally Yupscale. The days when you could have a beer at Moe's & Joe's while waiting for your clothes to dry at the Laundromat across the street are long gone. The Laundromat is now a boutique. Moe's & Joe's has patio seating and a clientele too young to remember that this used to be a biker hangout. In the old neighborhood's place is a trendy drag that has become one of Atlanta's leading attractions, bustling with stores, restaurants, bars, and enough coffee houses (4) to give espresso a buzz. Parking is a major problem. Find a street spot off the main drag (the intersection of Virginia and Highland avenues) and pick your destination. Bars and restaurants abound in the 4-block heart of the district. They include Moe's & Joe's, Everybody's Pizza, Murphy's, Capos, Chow, The Dessert Place, Taco Macs and Aurora Coffee. Fueled and ready to shop, check out Affairs (1401 N. Highland Ave.) gift shop; 20th Century (1044 N. Highland Ave.), an antique store specializing in art deco items and international antiques; Antiques Inc. (1003 Virginia Ave.), specializing in campy collectibles; Mitzi & Romano (1038 N. Highland Ave.), a women's designer boutique; and Mooncakes (1019 Virginia Ave), a women's boutique with an international flavor that offers everything from sexy lingerie to mukluks from Pakistan.

Virginia-Highlands, corner of Virginia and Highland avenues, about 5 miles northeast of downtown.

61 / 7-Bar Blues

Blind Willie's

If you want to hear the blues, you're gonna have to pay your dues to get into this shoe box-sized club that defies the tony Virginia-Highlands neighborhood where it's stashed (next to a laundrette) a few doors from its flashier, ultra-trendy neighbors, the Dark Horse Tavern and Surin of Thailand. By the time the music cranks up late on weekends, patrons are lined up on the street hoping for a seat at hard tables in extremely cramped quarters. Since its opening in 1986, the club—named after famed Atlanta bluesman "Blind" Willie McTell—has become the favorite of local blues devotees, scenesters and visiting musicians (Mink Jagger usually makes a point of dropping in when the Rolling Stones are in town). Crowds cover the waterfront from Yups to Grunge. The club sells beer, wine, mixed drinks, and bar food (chicken wings, sandwiches), but music is the draw. Owners Eric King (a former blues DJ on Atlanta counter-culture station WRFG-93 FM), and Roger Gregory have shown an impeccable eye for budding blues talent. They've helped launch the careers of such local acts as Luther "Houserooker" Johnson and Sandra Hall and the Excellos, who are regular house acts. The club is a regular stop for touring musicians, offering patrons every shade of blues, from New Orleans-style (Roulettes) to Texas kick-out-the-slats riffs of Johnny Copeland, both of whom have performed here. Seating is so cramped (most of it smack up against the stage) you'll feel like you're performing along with them. The noise? What? Loud! The later it gets, the louder it gets. To get a seat, the earlier you arrive the better. Have a drink while you wait, and be sure to get all your talking done while it's still possible. If you arrive late, don't despair. While you're waiting, you can get a buzz just hanging out on the sidewalk.

Virginia-Highlands

Blind Willie's, 828 North Highland Avenue; (404) 873-2583. Hours: Monday-Sunday 8:00 p.m.-2:00 a.m. Music cranks up at 10:00 p.m. No reservations, and the cover charge varies widely depending upon the band.

62 / Where Is That Nobel Peace Prize?

The Carter Presidential Center

The Carter Presidential Center is the home of the Jimmy Carter Library and Museum and provides visitors with an insight into the complex problems and issues faced by the person who sits in the White House. Elected as the 39th President of the United States in 1976, Jimmy Carter's roots run deep in Georgia soil. He was a peanut farmer from Plains, Ga., when he was elected state senator and governor of Georgia. Since the end of his presidency, he has earned respect and admiration for his humanitarian work and efforts as an international peacemaker. On display are memorabilia and writings revealing much about the character of the man and how his principles helped shape his decisions. There is a 30-minute film about the presidency and an interactive video that allows visitors to experience a question-and-answer session with President Carter in a "town meeting" format. Exhibits include a replica of the Oval Office, photographs and displays focusing on Carter's accomplishments since leaving office. Carter intended this center to be more than just a library of his papers. This is the focal point for his ongoing involvement in numerous social and environmental issues. As a result, exhibits are always being changed and updated and guest lecturers appear on a periodic basis. The Carter Center is surrounded by fountains and gardens and can be a pleasant place to have lunch. The Copenhill Cafe in the museum offers soups and sandwiches at reasonable prices. The Carter Center is found off Freedom Parkway one mile from Downtown Atlanta and is easily accessible by car. The route is well marked with large signs, and there is ample free parking available. A stop here will make you wonder why anyone would really want this job—and, perhaps, make you admire those who've taken it on. *Virginia-Highlands*

The Carter Presidential Center, 441 Freedom Parkway; (404) 331-0296. Hours: Monday-Saturday 9:00 a.m.-4:45 p.m., Sunday noon-4:45 p.m. Admission: adults $4, seniors $3, children and youth under 16 free.

63 / Heningway on the Half-shell

Indigo Coastal Grill

Atlanta's land-locked diners have long found their beach fix at Indigo Coastal Grill, a faux Key West restaurant in Virginia-Highlands that, as much as any eatery in town, helped launch the city's restaurant boom in the early 1980s. For a decade it has set and held the standard for casual, hip dining with a style verging on the camp and cuisine that is consistently fresh, inventive and superb. By turns, and by the diner's mood, it can be romantic, intimate, boisterous and just plain a hoot. The restaurant has the feel of a battered beach house, with a Caribbean pastel color scheme of coral walls, turquoise beamed ceiling, overhead fans and an open kitchen. A huge aquarium with brilliant tropical fish greets the visitor at the front door, and the back porch is sheltered with a canvas awning. Tables are candlelit and covered with brown butcher paper. The crowd is mixed: Yuppies, artists, media types and neighborhood regulars. Unless you arrive early, you can expect to have to wait for a table, so have a drink at the bar. Indigo pours strong drinks and one of the best Margaritas in town. The food is excellent all the way down the menu, and nightly specials are listed on chalk boards. Make sure you leave enough room for Indigo's dessert specialty: Key Lime pie.

Virginia-Highlands

Indigo Coastal Grill, 1397 North Highland Avenue; (404) 876-0676. Hours: Dinner Monday-Saturday 5:30-11:00 p.m., Sunday 9:00 a.m.-3:00 p.m.

64 / Curry Your Way

Surin of Thailand

Cozy, warm, elegant and romantic, Surin takes Thai cuisine and style up another level. The storefront restaurant in Atlanta's popular Virginia-Highlands neighborhood is tastefully decorated with royal blue satin tablecloths, candles and flowers at every table, pressed tin ceiling, and sunny pastel walls decorated with colorful photographs of Thailand. On crowded weekends the noise level can reach quite a din. But the stylish crowd Surin attracts finds the hustle and bustle part of the appeal, along with brisk service and a menu which, entrée to entrée, is fresh, delicious, and full of surprises. People travel miles for the fresh basil rolls. They are light, moist (in rice paper rolls), crisp, and come with a spicy plum sauce. The mee-krob (crunchy noodles prepared in a tamarind sauce with shrimp, eggs and bean sprouts as a garnish) are equally compelling. For soup, try the spicy hot and sour shrimp soup, which serves two. Among the recommended entrées: chicken curry, pungent, rich, velvety and mildly hot; chicken panany, prepared in a red curry paste sautéed with coconut milk, chili peppers, lime peel and basil; and Pad Prick, a sumptuously tangy mingling of green beans, curry and chicken, beef or pork. For a beverage, try the Thai Iced Tea (a blend of herb tea and cream on ice). Dessert? You can't go wrong with any of four ice creams made on the premises: coconut, mango, great tea, or ginger. Reservation's aren't accepted, so on weekends expect a 30- to 45-minute wait.

Virginia-Highlands

Surin of Thailand, 810 North Highland Ave.; (404) 892-7789. Hours: Monday-Thursday 11:30 am-10:00 p.m., Friday 11:30 a.m-11:30 p.m., Saturday noon-11:30 p.m., Sunday, noon-10:00 p.m.

65 / The Wide World of Beer

Taco Mac

There are a number of Taco Macs in Atlanta, but there may be no better spot for hot wings and cold beer than the Virginia-Highlands location. This is the original Taco Mac, opened since 1979, and it has something of a grungy, bohemian look. With one glance, a sign in the back of your mind begins to flash "hot wings." Seating, inside and on the patio, is on high bar chairs at small tables, but anything else would be wrong. The menu offers sandwiches, Mexican dishes and salads (if you must), but it is the wings that draw you in. Mild, medium and hot are all excellent. If you are one of those people who think chicken wings can't be made too hot for you, then you are in for a challenge: The "Three Mile Island" wings (yes, they were named for the nuclear meltdown) will set you free. The beer selection is not what you would call limited. Listed are 338 brands from countries all over the world allowing you to try such exotic offerings as Mamba (Ivory Coast), Golden Eagle (India), or Brahma (Brazil). Taco Macs tends to be crowded, especially on weekends, and tables on the patio are usually at a premium during nice weather. A double order of hot wings and a few Mambas will jump start your evening on the town.

Virginia-Highlands

Taco Mac, 1006 North Highland Ave.; (404) 873-6529. Hours: Monday-Saturday 10:00-2:00 a.m., Sunday 11:00-2:00 a.m.

66 / The Scruffy Side of the Street

Poncey-Highlands

The district between Little Five Points and Virginia-Highlands, known to locals as Poncey-Highlands, gets overlooked in most guidebooks because, well, it tends toward squalor. The derelict elements remain. One needs only take a peek in the Clermont Lounge—one of Atlanta's rougher strip joints—to confirm it will be a while before this section of Atlanta makes the Chamber's highlight reel. But, like the neighborhoods around it, Poncey-Highlands has been on the mend over the last decade. Parts of the 6-block neighborhood are downright Yuppy. To get there, head east on Ponce de Leon off Peachtree to the 700 block of Ponce, marked by Green's Liquor Store on the right. Park on a side street and walk. The neighborhood's more interesting spots include Dugan's Tavern, a popular late-night club with outdoor seating and pool tables; Jave Jive, a pseudo-diner with funky formica-highlighted decor; Tortillas, which serves fresh, inexpensive Mexican food with pleasant open-air seating upstairs; and the venerable Majestic Food Shop, the ne plus ultra of divey Atlanta diners. In the wee hours, the Majestic is one of the wildest people-watching spots in Atlanta, a veritable Zoo Atlanta with hashbrowns on the side. If it's very late and you're very whatever, drop in.

Dugan's Tavern, 777 Ponce de Leon Ave. N.E.; (404) 885-1217.

Java Jive, 790 Ponce de Leon Ave., N.E.; (404) 876-6161.

Tortillas, 774 Ponce de Leon Ave. N.E.; (404) 892-3493.

Majestic Food Shop, 1031 Ponce de Leon Ave. N.E.; (404) 875-0276.

67 / Bohemians on Holiday

Little Five Points

Little Five Points is Atlanta's most bohemian neighborhood, the city's SoHo, a place where hippies refuse to die, eating meat packs a moral consequence, and a skinhead is a lot more than just a bad haircut. Atlantans and tourists flock here on weekends just to soak up the scene. The heart of the neighborhood, the corner of Moreland and Euclid avenues, teems with all forms of urban street life: youth sprouting jewelry from every visible appendage; aging '60s flower children; goateed beatnik types, bikers, skinheads, street musicians and shoppers just looking for a good time or great deals at a variety of bars and live music clubs, second-hand stores, specialty shops, art galleries, book stores and boutiques. Among the most popular haunts: **Stefan's** (1160 Euclid Ave.), a second-hand store which sells vintage clothes from the 1890s to the 1960s; **Rene Rene** (1142 Euclid Ave.), the city's leading offbeat women's boutique; **Throb** (1140 Euclid Ave.), outfitter for the city's more daring night crawlers, with lots of leather, minis, and outrageous jewelry; **A Cappella Books** (1113 Euclid Ave.), an offbeat bookstore specializing in out-of-print titles; **Berman Gallery** (1131 Euclid Ave.), specializing in folk artists (such as Howard Finster) and rustic pottery; **African Connections** (1107 Euclid Ave.), which carries authentic clothes and jewelry imported from Africa **Wax 'N' Facs** (423 Moreland Ave. N.E.), an offbeat music store that sells new and vintage albums, tapes and CDs. Live avant guarde music can be heard nightly at **The Point** (420 Moreland Ave. N.E.); or there's **Good Ol' Days** (401 Moreland Ave. N.E.) for the folkie crowd.

68 / Tom Wolfe and a Cup of Joe

Cafe Diem

This delightful international coffeehouse on the fringe of Virginia-Highlands is a great place to stop for a late-night cup of coffee, dinner or one of the city's better, off-beat Sunday brunches. In fact, off-beat is the only beat this smallish but not cramped restaurant marches to. The decor is airy and light (pastel yellow walls decorated with ethnic art of uncertain pedigree, tile floor, small linen-top tables), even if the crowd tends to struggling artists and tortured poets. They're integral to Cafe Diem's brooding, Greewich Village charm. On the first Tuesday of every month, the cafe hosts poetry readings with changing themes. But even starving artists eventually eat, and, attendant to the cafe's invigorating selection of coffees—Latte Doppio, Mochaccino Blanc and, a favorite, Mocha au Lait (strong black coffee served in a bowl-sized cup with a side of steaming chocolate milk)—are delectable appetizers. The hummus, served with toasted pita bread, is tangy and rich. Tamenade toasts—hot French bread toasted, crunchy, and exotic, answer to pizza by the slice. Try the filling and flavorful Diem combo sandwich, a healthy combination of ham, turkey, and Provolone cheese on a baguette with tomato, sprouts, and vinaigrette dressing. For dessert, try the intoxicating Snickers, cheesecake, with chocolate crust, caramel-coated and sprinkled with peanuts. Many regulars save their appetite for Sunday brunch, when the restaurant offers sumptuous and inventive variations on Eggs Benedict.

Little Five Points

Cafe Diem, 640 North Highland Avenue.; (404) 607-7008. Hours: Monday 3:00 p.m.-12:00 a.m., Tuesday-Thursday 11:30-12:00 a.m., Friday 11:30-2:00 a.m., Saturday 11:00-2:00 a.m., Sunday 11:00-12:00 a.m. No reservations.

69 / The Only Real Bar in Atlanta
Manuel's Tavern

Regulars will tell you Manuel's is the only REAL tavern in Atlanta. Since the regulars here have sampled a few, it's best not to argue. They're probably right, anyway. This sprawling "smoky dive"—as it was unceremoniously described in *The Wall Street Journal*—is the Big Daddy of Atlanta beer joints and the most democratic place in the city to munch bar food, toss down boiled peanuts and consort with buddies. Owned by former DeKalb County Commissioner Manuel Maloof, it's the haunt of politicos (President Clinton dropped by while in town; former president Jimmy Carter, whose Carter Center is around the corner, is a regular), journalists, writers, lawyers, college students, artists, blue-collar workers, professionals and off-duty cops. They don't come here for the decor, which is as studied as a three-car pile-up (check out the nude painting over the bar, which, as the story goes, Maloof bought for $150 from an artist customer who needed the dough and didn't mind his wife hanging around a bar naked). The bar, while it can get rowdy on Friday and Saturday nights, is as safe for single men as women. What little cruising there is takes place in the main bar, where barkeep McClosky strictly enforces the speed limit. Mostly, this is a place where friends meet and ratiocinate (it is here that an Emory professor is said to have first articulated his theory that God is dead). In the spring, Manuel's hosts Shakespeare's plays in the back room; Thursday is improvisational comedy night. For sports fans, there's always a game playing on an array of TVs in each room. If you're in Atlanta long enough to visit one bar, this is IT.

Little Five Points

Manuel's Tavern, 602 North Highland Ave.; (404) 525-3447. Hours: Monday-Saturday, 11:00-2 a.m., Sunday, 3:00 p.m.-midnight.

70 / Nautical Nights
Euclid Avenue Yacht Club

On Sundays, the Euclid Avenue Yacht Club looks a fright. Is somebody shooting a remake of *The Wild One*? Dozens of Harleys are parked out front, and inside the dress du jour is leather. But peaceful coexistence prevails. This is Little Five Points, a section where opposing points—bikers, punks, poets, street people, bohemians and dissolutes—meet but seldom collide. The Yacht Club is where the scene moves indoors, the later the better. Cramped, raucous, and whimsically appointed (fishnets dangle from the ceiling, stuffed bass stare from the walls, there's an aquarium over the beer cooler), the Yacht Club takes some things seriously, however. It serves the best kosher hot dogs and Philly cheese steaks in town. But the bar's real hook is its atmosphere. On weekends, especially late, the place jumps with a mostly very young, very hip, very beery crowd dancing to loud music on the juke box, banging elbows in the cramped main room, or just making the scene in the adjoining dining area where the large clamorous tables are usually jammed. Come prepared to stand. Making conversation is possible, but not likely. This is a great place to get wound up while you're winding down. Just sit back and soak up the wild surf of this club as it crashes over you.

Little Five Points

Euclid Avenue Yacht Club, 1136 Euclid Avenue, N.E.; (404) 688-2582. Hours: Monday-Sunday noon-2:00 a.m.

71 / The Heart of Atlanta
Tanyard Branch Creek Park

If Oakland Cemetery is the soul of Atlanta, then Tanyard Branch Creek Park is the heart, the ground upon which was fought the Battle of Peachtree Creek, the first and most decisive engagement of Confederate and Union forces in the siege of Atlanta. Five days before the battle, Confederate President Jefferson Davis relieved General Joseph E. Johnson of the command of the Confederate army in Atlanta and placed it under General J.B. Hood. Davis had grown impatient with Johnson's tactics of defending against rather than attacking Sherman, whose army outnumbered Johnson's almost 2 to 1. Under Hood, the Confederates took the initiative, attacking about 4:30 in the afternoon of July 20, 1864, hoping to catch Union forces off guard as they forded Peachtree Creek. Had they attacked at noon as originally planned, the Confederates might have succeeded. Instead, the delayed attack in three sorties across Peachtree Creek was brutally repelled, the fiercest fighting taking place at Tanyard Branch. By nightfall 4,796 Confederate and 1,710 Union troops lay dead. Two days later, near the intersection of what is now I-20 and Memorial Drive, the Confederates were defeated at the Battle of Atlanta, losing 7,000 troops to the Union's 2,000. For the next month, Federal forces rained cannon fire on the civilian population, forcing Hood to retreat and Atlanta to surrender on Sept. 2. The visitor interested in exploring the war that did so much to define Atlanta will find Tanyard Creek Park the best site within the city to walk a relatively unspoiled battleground. Historical markers at the entry to the park, pointing out troop movements, will enable the visitor, with a little imagination, to envision the pivotal battle. Atlantans have come here and wept.

Tanyard Branch Creek Park is a quarter of a mile west of Peachtree Street on Collier Rd., just north of Midtown.

72 / Best Greyhounds in Town
Houston's

Houston's is a chair restaurant but there ends the link to its fern-bar kin. Located almost exactly between Midtown and the heart of Buckhead in the fashionable Peachtree Battle neighborhood, it's a great, lively spot for dinner or a quick lunch for shoppers perusing the specialty stores on nearby Bennett Street. The dimly-lit interior, accented with brick walls and flickering lamps in a gaslight-district motif, is brightened by a frenetic open kitchen and a glassed-in bar that overlooks Peachtree Street and Houston's patio seating. In the expansive yet cozy dining room, seating is in comfortable upholstered booths with tiny brass table lamps. Service from the young, sharply attired staff (starched white shirts, blue and red ties, khaki slacks) is brisk and unfailingly courteous. Across the menu, grilled fish, beef, and chicken dishes are consistently superb. On weekend nights when waits are an hour or longer, consider eating at the bar. Recommended grazing food: the Chicago-style spinach and artichoke dip (maybe not balanced but a meal in itself) and the loaded baked potato. Entrées include Houston's famous "knife-and-fork ribs," served in full and half slabs (arguably the best in town); the Santa Fe platter (grilled chicken breast with tomatoes, onion, zucchini, cilantro, and goat cheese-seared tuna salad, served with cilantro ginger vinaigrette, tossed greens, and avocado). Houston's also offers a delicious Thai chicken pizza, with grilled chicken, mozzarella, chopped cilantro and light peanut sauce. For dessert, two favorites: Key lime pie and five-nut brownie, served á la mode with Kahlua. Houston's also serves one of the best hot weather drinks in the world, the greyhound: fresh squeezed grapefruit juice and vodka served over cracked ice.

Peachtree-Battle

Houston's, 2166 Peachtree Road.; (404) 351-2442. Hours: Sunday-Thursday 11:00 a.m.-11:00 p.m., Friday-Saturday 11:00 a.m.-midnight. No reservations.

73 / Antique and Art Bazaar

Bennett Street

Bennett Street used to host one of Atlanta's liveliest bar scenes. But as clubs such as the Surf Club, Harrison's and Uncle Sam's came and went over the years, Bennett Street evolved into one of the city's more popular shopping districts for collectors of art and antiques. Begin your treasure hunt at the Tula Arts Complex (located near the foot of this dead-end street), a warehouse partitioned into more than a dozen art galleries and studios where visitors can watch artists at work. The nearby Cricket Gallery offers animation cell art at a price; Evelyn Hammond exhibits hand-painted photographs; and the artist-owned Ariel Gallery shows paintings and sculpture by Atlanta artists. The Lowe Gallery occupies the largest space in the complex and sells its priciest pieces: check out the mural-size paintings for $12,000 and up. Next door, the Interiors Market houses more than 30 antique dealers and a trendy coffee/sandwich shop, Bella Cucina. Other intriguing galleries and antique dealers along the street include Nottingham Antiques, The Stalls, Folk Art Imports Gallery, and many others. You can easily burn up an afternoon (and your budget) browsing on Bennett Street. If you plan to do more than look, bring plenty of cash or plastic. This is no flea market. Bennett Street is located off Peachtree Street and hours vary from store to store, so call ahead.

Peachtree-Battle

Tula Arts Complex, 75 Bennett Street N.W.,; (404) 351-3551.

Interiors Market, 55 Bennett Street N.W.; (404) 352-0055.

Nottingham Antiques, 45 Bennett Street N.W.; (404) 352-1890.

The Stalls, 116 Bennett Street N.W.; (404) 352-4430.

Folk Art Imports Gallery, 25 Bennett Street N.W.; (404) 352-2656.

74 / Kings—and Queens—of Comedy
Comedy Clubs

Everybody wants to be a comedian—just look at Congress. The explosion of comedy clubs in cities across the country has provided the Big Break for many new and successful entertainers; it has also subjected audiences to some horrid attempts at humor. Atlanta is no exception. There are a number of comedy clubs scattered throughout the city, and the entertainment offered is diverse and ever changing. On stage, you'll find everybody from top professionals to rank, and we do mean rank, amateurs. Basically, "you pays yo' money and takes yo' chances." Two of the best clubs the city has to offer are The Punchline and the Uptown Comedy Corner. The Punchline (in Sandy Springs, a suburb north of Atlanta) serves dinner with the show, and on Thursdays and Fridays has no-smoking shows. Reservations are required and should be made at least 24 hours in advance. The Uptown Comedy Corner offers a buffet and has a two-drink minimum. The best advance is check a local entertainment guide to see who is playing and call for admission and show times. Although it is not a comedy club, Manuel's Tavern (see separate listing) showcases the Laughing Matters improvisational group on Thursday and Saturday nights and is well worth seeing. Again, call for reservations.

The Punchline, 280 Hilderbrand Drive, Sandy Springs, GA 30328; (404) 252-5233. Call for show times, admission rates and reservations. *Sandy Springs*

Uptown Comedy Corner, 2140 Peachtree Road; (404) 350-6990. Call for show times, admission rates and reservations. *Peachtree-Battle*

75 / Happy Hour for the Health Conscious

Cochran Shoals Park

In the afternoons during warm weather, this park is Atlanta's happy hour for the healthy, and one of the city's most breathless singles scenes. What more could you ask than this visual "twofer"—unspoiled river vistas and gaspy views of some of the city's most heavenly bodies; jogging, cycling, strolling or just checking out the action. The 108-acre park on the Chattahoochee River, smack in the middle of South Cobb County's vital and affluent neighborhood of young singles, features a 3.3-mile jogging and bike trail and a fitness course where the health nut can get in the requisite pull-ups, crunches, dips and stretching exercises. Bring along your dog and try that old urban dog-walker's gambit: "Is that a Shih Tzu, or is he walking backwards?" Or just commune with nature, toss a Frisbee, or gather wool by the riverbank. Serious athletes are welcome, but it's better to come in the early morning on weekdays when it's less crowded. You might meet one of Atlanta's overachievers running off yesterday's power lunch (Home Depot president and Outward Bound devotee, Arthur Blank, is a regular here). During afternoons and on weekends, this is more a place to be seen. The parking lot is overflowing and the trail is so packed that making a brisk run, dodging people, bikes, dogs, and parents with strollers is more like a treacherous downhill slalom. The park is part of the Chattahoochee River National Recreation Area.

Peachtree-Battle

Cochran Shoals Park, Interstate North Parkway (I-285 to Exit 15, then north; (404) 395-8335. Hours: generally sunrise to sunset, but hours vary according to the season.

76 / Italian Cuisine in a Romantic Setting

Abruzzi

Atlanta culinary awakening in the 1980s is best reflected in the array of first-rate Italian restaurants, none more consistently delightful than Abruzzi. Obscured in the Peachtree-Battle Shopping Center (a few doors down from a hardware store), Abruzzi rises above its humble appearance. Inside, the diner is transported to a world with the elegant and romantic appeal of a posh Manhattan restaurant. The color scheme, peach and green fabric walls, white linen tablecloths and seating (banquettes along both walls and small tables in the center) impart a coziness that segues to intimacy as diners settle in to be pampered by a kitchen that encourages ordering nonmenu items and a wait staff that is attentive and superbly versed in the ample wine list offered and the nuances of Italian cuisine. The ambience has prompted more than one fellow to pop THE question and this is, without peer, the place for Valentines and romantics. Even with reservations, you can expect a short wait. Recommended appetizers: smoked salmon garnished with red onions and capers; escargot sautéed with fresh mint, tomato and brandy; baked eggplant stuffed with spinach and cheese. For entrees, you can't go wrong with the daily specials (pumpkin ravioli), and the quail, when offered, is excellent. For the adventurous, Abruzzi serves game, venison, rabbit and wild boar. Save some room for dessert; Abruzzi serves the city's best tiramisu.

Peachtree-Battle

Abruzzi, 2355 Peachtree Road; (404) 261-8186. Hours: Monday-Friday lunch 11:30 a.m.-2:30 p.m., dinner Monday-Thursday 5:45-10:30 p.m., Friday-Saturday 5:45-11:30 p.m. Reservations recommended.

77 / Southern Bookstore with a New York Flavor

Oxford Books

Bookstores and newsstands abound in Atlanta, but one would be hard pressed to find a wider selection of new and used volumes than in Peachtree-Battle shopping center at Oxford Books and its partner in tomes, Oxford Too. When major retailers such as Barnes & Noble and Borders can't locate the volume you're looking for, they invariably suggest Oxford. Tucked into a corner of the open-air shopping center, it's the city's closest approximation to a New York book store. On Sundays, customers comb racks for their favorite out-of-town Sunday newspapers, then amble upstairs to peruse it in the on-premises coffee shop, the Cup and Chaucer. The Cup and Chaucer serves a variety of bracing brews, pastries and bagels to accompany your absorbing read. Oxford is open late and has become a meeting place for booklovers who are looking for someone to read with. (If you happen to meet someone, do not start the conversation by saying you have seen the movie.) Oxford Too is a short walk across the parking lot. This large and rambling store contains thousands of volumes, both new and used. It is easy to lose several hours just wandering the stacks. There is a section for early editions and rare prints. They also offer a tracking service for locating out-of-print books. Oxford has several other locations, each offering something special, but the two stores at Peachtree-Battle can save a lot of travel time for the center-city visitor looking to browse.

Peachtree-Battle

Oxford Books, 2345 Peachtree Rd.; (404) 364-2700. Hours: Sunday-Thursday, 9:00 a.m.-midnight, Friday and Saturday, 9:00-1:00 a.m. The Cup and Chaucer opens at the same time the store does but closes one hour earlier.

Oxford Too, 2395 Peachtree Rd.; (404) 262-3411. Hours: Sunday-Thursday, 9:00 a.m.-10:00 p.m., Friday and Saturday, 9:00 a.m.-midnight.

78 / Joel Chandler Harris Museum

The Wren's Nest

While the name Joel Chandler Harris may stir only a vague recollection somewhere in the back of your mind, the mention of Uncle Remus is certain to jog childhood memories. The wonderful stories of Br'er Rabbit and Br'er Fox are a staple of children's bedtime stories and The Wren's Nest is where Harris, Georgia's Aesop, created his cast of characters. Along with Mark Twain, Harris has from time to time come under attack by revisionists who judged the period language of his stories derogatory to African Americans. The prevailing attitude today, however, is that Harris was one of the first writers to chronicle African folk tales that had been handed down from generation to generation via oral history. This Victorian cottage has been restored and is very much the same as when Harris, a columnist for the *Atlanta Constitution*, began writing the Uncle Remus tales for the paper in 1878. Harris lived here from 1881 until his death in 1908 and wrote many of the stories in a rocking chair on the front porch. By the time of his death, his fame was such that President Theodore Roosevelt came to Atlanta to raise money for a memorial at Wren's Nest. A visit to The Wren's Nest is not complete without experiencing the storytelling sessions. They're what give The Wren's Nest its special charm and are well worth the additional $2 above the admission price. During Christmas the cottage is decorated with period ornaments, and on the Sunday closest to Harris's birthday (December 9), there is an open house. Plan to spend an hour or so at The Wren's Nest in order to enjoy the tour and storytelling.

West End

The Wren's Nest, 1050 Ralph David Abernathy Blvd.; (404) 753-7735. Hours: Tuesday-Saturday 10:00 a.m.-4:00 p.m., Sunday 1:00-4:00 p.m. Closed Mondays. Admission: adults $4, seniors and teens $3, children 4 through 12 $2; storytelling sessions are an additional $2.

79 / Hong Kong in the South
Honto

For years Honto has been known as the best Chinese restaurant in Atlanta, but, until recently, it was only for those who preferred their Hong Kong-style fish house cuisine a little TOO authentic. Cleanliness was not always a top priority; service could be surly. These days the bustling restaurant has been spruced up and diners no longer need to speak in native Chinese to get acceptable (if not stellar) service. There are a few trappings of typical American-Chinese restaurants. Honto's two sprawling dining rooms are separated by gold carved wood arches; the back wall sports the gold dragon/red fabric motif indigenous to the city's tamer Chinese kin. The resemblance ends there. Most nights the crowd—a mixture of Chinese-speaking immigrants from the local melting-pot neighborhood, college kids, yupsters, blue-collar types, and Atlantans lucky enough to have found this jewel buried in the 'burbs—is loud and overflowing. If you want to play it safe and soak up the atmosphere, order off the Cantonese (tourist) menu. For a wilder ride, order off the smaller Hong Kong menu. Favorites include the salt-and-pepper squid (tossed with bell and Jalapeño peppers, served steaming hot); pan-fried Pompano in a light, gingery soy sauce with green onions and clams steamed in garlic butter with cilantro-spiced broth, soft-shell crabs with ginger and green onions, and a side of black-bean sauce (salty and piquant). Regulars love an afternoon of Dim Sum (Chinese tea lunch), where diners pick from a vast array of appetizer-sized dishes ferried to tables on carts.
Chamblee

Honto, 3295 Chamblee-Dunwoody Road, Chamble, GA 30341; (404) 458-8088. Hours: Monday-Thursday 11:30 a.m.-9:45 p.m., Friday 11:30 a.m.-11:00 p.m., Saturday-Sunday 11:00-2:00 a.m. Dim Sum served Saturday-Monday 11:00 a.m.-2:00 p.m. No reservations.

80 / A Place to Prowl for Secrets

The Book Nook

When you walk into the Book Nook, you feel as if you've been given permission to pilfer in the attic of grandpa's house. Books, videos, records, tapes, CDs, comics and collectible toys are simply everywhere. Most items are used, and there is a definite flea market atmosphere here. Books and records are supposedly arranged, but the order may elude you. However, you browse with a purpose because you know a treasure may just be on the next shelf. The Book Nook offers one of the finest collections of books on music and pop culture you will find anywhere in the city. There is also an excellent science fiction and comic book section. The old barter system of buy, sell and trade is alive and well here, so don't be afraid to make an offer. Prices are generally reasonable, and there's always a chance to make a deal. The Book Nook is not the kind of place you want to just drop by for a minute because there is too much to take in. This is browser's heaven.

Chamblee

The Book Nook, 3342 Clairmont Road; (404) 633-1328. Hours: open seven days a week 10:00 a.m.-10:30 p.m.

81 / 175 TVs . . . and Everyone On
Frankie's Food, Sports, and Spirits

Frankie's no longer carries blacked-out Atlanta Falcon's games; the NFL cracked down on the practice last season, fining three sports bars in the city. The Falcons finished their usual, and dreadful, 7-9 (thank you, NFL), but Frankie's is doing just fine. The bar, a sprawling paean to the marvels of satellite dishes (12 on the roof feed 175 TVs every conceivable sports broadcast, from football to water-skiing championships), is Atlanta's biggest and busiest sports bar—in the evenings a sizzling singles scene and on weekends the home of a dozen fan clubs who congregate to watch games they can't get at home. On the back wall in the main room a floor-to-ceiling video bank beams featured games whose players seem nearly life-size. Even if you're not here to watch a game (though it's unavoidable), the bar features enough sports memorabilia to make a visit worthwhile. More than 1,000 sports photographs, many of them signed, adorn the walls. An abundance of framed, signed game jerseys (Michael Jordan, Wayne Gretzky), and other sports collectibles fill in what space remains. Is it any wonder *USA Today* named Frankie's one of the nations Top 10 sports bars? Frankie's serves a good hamburger with a side of tasty beer-battered French fries and the usual assortment of bar food. Local sports stars can be seen here on a regular basis, and visiting heroes have dropped in, too. In warmer weather you can sit out on the patio (don't worry, plenty of TVs there, too). If you're a sports junkie, Frankie's is the place in Atlanta to get your fix.
Sandy Springs

Frankie's Food Sports and Spirits, 5600 Roswell Road; (404) 843-9444. Hours: Sunday-Thursday 11:00-2:00 a.m., Saturday and Sunday 11:00-3:00 a.m.

82 / House of the Original Chick-fil-A Sandwich

Dwarf House Restaurant

Unlike Coca-Cola, there is no World of Chick-fil-A. Maybe that's because watching the assembly of a chicken sandwich just isn't as fascinating as watching Coca-Cola bottles rattle by on an assembly line. Instead, the humble beginnings from which Chick-fil-A launched its region-wide chicken sandwich chain remain humble. The first store, the Dwarf House Restaurant in Hapeville, south of downtown, reminds you of one of those old-fashioned diners you used to see in the movies of the 1950s. It is not big or fancy by any standard, but the restaurant is clean, neat and appealing. Seating is limited to ten booths or a stool at the counter and during lunch or dinner hours you can expect to wait. Service is as brisk and friendly as at a '50s carhop. In addition to the famed Chick-fil-A sandwich (battered-fried, on a bun, with a pickle), the restaurant serves an outstanding Dwarfburger (it's more than just another hamburger and dwarf in name only). The Chick-fil-A plate (the way to go) is best accompanied with a large sweet tea. (It's one of those things that doesn't go better with coke.) Afterward, have a slice of pie or a cup of Ice Dream, ice cream that is as close to homemade as you will find. There are a number of Dwarf House restaurants in the metro area and practically every mall has a Chick-fil-A outlet. Somehow the original just makes things taste better.

Southside

Dwarf House Restaurant, 461 S. Central Avenue, Hapevill, GA 30354; (404) 762-1746. Hours: Monday-Saturday open 24 hours a day. Closes at 4:00 a.m. Sunday and reopens at 5:00 a.m. Monday.

83 / A Good Place to Take Your Spring Break

Spondivits

If you long for the days of beaches and cold beer, when the first inkling of warm weather made you want to seek the ocean, then Spondivits should be a definite stop. This tavern sits incongruously between a McDonald's and a Waffle House, but do not let the location fool you. Inside is a little bit of Florida, complete with cold beer served in frosted mugs and terrific shellfish. The menu offers something for everyone, but regulars favor the steamed oysters and bucket of crab, lobster or shrimp. If you decide to drink only one beer, the 33-ounce mug of draft is the answer. The walls are adorned with marine bric-a-brac and there are numerous televisions scattered about if you feel the need to watch the game du jour. You can nurse a cocktail and watch the inhabitants in one of the two 250-plus-gallon aquariums and wonder if they are actually studying you. There is an outside patio that can be wonderful in the summer. This is not a large place and tends to be crowded late in the evening, especially on weekends; you may have to wait for a table. On some occasions live music is offered but there usually is no cover or minimum. *One note:* Seafood in Atlanta is generally expensive and can fluctuate based on the market price of the season. A combo bucket, a mixed pound of shrimp, crab legs and lobster tails, will run around $21.95. Located on the southside of Atlanta near the airport, Spondivits is the best place in Atlanta to pretend you're on spring break. A beer and a bucket and you can almost hear the ocean.

Southside

Spondivits, 1219 Virginia Ave.; (404) 767-1551. Hours: Monday-Saturday 11:00-4:00 a.m.; Sunday noon-4:00 a.m.; Food served until 2:00 a.m.

84 / Home to Endangered Species

Zoo Atlanta

Zoo Atlanta was once one of the most shameful and despicable institutions of its kind in the country. A former employee was even accused of taking sick animals home, putting them out of their misery—and then having them for dinner. But thanks to dynamic leadership and aggressive fund raising in recent years, Atlanta now has one of the top-rated zoos in the nation. Gone are rows of cramped cages in favor of large, natural outdoor habitats that allow animals to roam much as they would in the wild. Over 1,000 specimens representing animals from all over the world can be observed living in naturalistic environments. Zoo Atlanta is heavily involved in research and the protection of endangered species. As a result you have the opportunity to see such rare animals as the Sumatran tiger, black rhino and Komodo monitor lizard. The most famous resident of Zoo Atlanta is the western lowland gorilla, Willie B. Named for former Mayor William B. Hartsfield, Willie B. has been a fixture in Atlanta since 1961. He lived alone until 1989, and when Willie B. finally had his first "date," it made national news. He is now the proud papa of baby Kudzu. Regular zoo events include a wildlife show, elephant show and daily animal feedings. (Call for scheduled times.) Zoo Atlanta offers numerous special events and programs throughout the year, many of them calling for advance registration. Again, call for details. The zoo continues to evolve and grow, and new exhibits are coming on display all the time. Zoo Atlanta is located in Grant Park just a few minutes from downtown and parking is free. The Cyclorama (see separate listing) is located adjacent to the zoo entrance. The combination of Cyclorama and zoo can make for a full day.

Grant Park

Zoo Atlanta, 800 Cherokee Avenue; Hours: Monday-Friday 10:00 a.m.-5:30 p.m., Saturday and Sunday 10:00 a.m.-6:30 p.m. Admission: adults $7.50, seniors $6.50, children 3-11 $5.

85 / Civil War Art

Cyclorama

The Civil War and Atlanta are never very far apart, and one of the most poignant reminders of that relationship is the Cyclorama. It took 11 German and Polish artists 22 months to complete the mammoth circular painting depicting the Battle of Atlanta, and from 1886 to 1891 it was displayed in cities throughout the country. It found a home in Atlanta in 1891 and has been at its current site in Grant Park since 1921. During the 1970s, the exhibit fell into serious disrepair. Fortunately, the historical and artistic importance of the Cyclorama was recognized before it was too late; the exhibit was saved through extensive renovation. The painting, which weighs 9,000 pounds, is 42 feet high and 358 feet in circumference. A diorama connects the canvas with the foreground and gives the viewer the feeling of being transported through time and put down in the middle of a battle that marked a turning point in the Civil War. Visitors view the Cyclorama from a theater-like auditorium which rotates, allowing the spectator to see the entire exhibit from one spot. A dramatic reading, complete with music and battle sounds, accompanies the viewing. The show lasts approximately 30 minutes, but you should allow at least one hour to see the full attraction. Also on display is the steam locomotive "Texas" along with photographs, paintings, uniforms, weaponry and various artifacts from the Civil War. The bookstore offers a wide selection of Civil War literature. If you enjoy history and the Civil War era or just want to see a remarkable work of art, make this one of your stops. The Cyclorama is adjacent to Zoo Atlanta; visits to both attractions can make for a full day.

Grant Park

Cyclorama, 800-C Cherokee Avenue; (404) 658-7625. Hours: seven day a week 9:30 a.m.-4:30 p.m. Admission: adults 13-59 $5, seniors $4, children 6-12 $3, children under 6 free with an adult.

86 / Heaven Sicilian-style

Jagger's

Best pizza in town, cold Bass Ale on tap and burgers hard to top (though the restaurant does, in five varieties) make Jagger's tavern a must for the famished traveler in search of good food and a little flashback college-bar atmosphere. The expanded hole-in-the-wall tavern in a retail strip across from the Emory University campus has been a favorite haunt of students, professionals, neighbors and blue-collar types for more than two decades. In that time, permutations of haute pizza have proliferated on menus across Atlanta, yet none has improved on Jagger's basic, cheesy, just-spicy-and-crusty-enough square of Sicilian-style heaven. The atmosphere is confortably dim, occasionally smoky (the added back room is nonsmoking), the decor a taverny mix of neon beer signs, old advertisements and movie posters. Pizza comes with the usual toppings (sorry, no barbecue or Thai). The restaurant also offers sandwiches, lasagna, sirloin tip pot roast, fried North Georgia rainbow trout, and a chicken finger platter. But if you're not up for pizza, we heartily recommend the hamburgers, which are as outstanding as the pizza. Hickory grilled to perfection and served with a side of French fries, they come basic or with five toppings (including a pizza burger for the indecisive). The Jagger's Patty Melt comes on grilled rye bread and its topped with sautéed onions and melted cheese. On weeknights, especially when school is out of session, crowds thin out. Watch a game at the bar or just sink into conversation about the "good ol' college days."

Emory

Jagger's, 1577 North Decatur Road; (404) 377-8888. Hours: Sunday 11:30 a.m.-9:00 p.m., Monday-Thursday 11:00 a.m.-1:00 p.m., Friday 11:00 a.m.-2:00 a.m., Saturday 11:00-1:00 a.m. No reservations.

87 / Stop and Smell the Roses
Atlanta Botanical Garden

If the boss has stomped on your last nerve and looking at the kids makes you understand why some animals eat their young, you need a few minutes to get back in touch with nature. There is no better place than the Atlanta Botanical Garden. The garden is divided into three main sections: a 15-acre hardwood forest, a landscape garden area and the 16,000-square-foot Dorothy Chapman Fuqua Conservatory. A walk through the hardwood forest is not overly difficult and can feel miles away from the city that is just a few blocks down the street. The garden area offers examples of landscaping that include a lovely Japanese garden, a rose garden and a rock garden. Fountains, ponds and statuary supplement many of the enchanting displays. There is a fragrance garden for the blind visitor, and the conservatory is home to almost every type of tropical plant and fern you can imagine. Some are extremely rare and are not likely to be seen elsewhere. The Atlanta Botanical Garden is open year round and enjoyable in all but the coldest weather. It's a good idea to wear comfortable shoes; once you get started, you may end up walking more than you had planned. It is also a good idea to take along pen and paper. You are almost certain to see something you would like to try in your own garden. There are also shows and lectures scheduled periodically throughout the year, so call ahead for a schedule of events. The Lanier Terrace Restaurant can be a great spot for that lunchtime picnic. Sandwiches and drinks can be purchased at reasonable prices and the smoked turkey sandwich ($5.50) is better than just good. The Garden Shop offers some terrific gift items. Guided tours are available for large groups with advance reservations.

Piedmont Park

Atlanta Botanical Garden, 1345 Piedmont Avenue; (404) 876-5859. Hours: garden Tuesday-Sunday 9:00 a.m.-6:00 p.m., conservatory and Garden Shop 10:00 a.m.-6:00 p.m. Closed Mondays. Lanier Terrace Restaurant 11:30 a.m.-2:00 p.m. Hours subject to change during summer months. Admission: adults $6, seniors $5, students $3, children under 6 free.

88 / Places to Stay on a Budget

Bed & Breakfast

Travelers seeking the comforts of home away from home probably will be disappointed by even the poshest of hotels. Their grandeur alone makes them impersonal. But, with enough advance planning, the traveler can book lodging at one of Atlanta's more than 100 bed and breakfasts. One of the best is the Ansley Inn, a restored Tudor mansion in fashionable Ansley Park. The inn is pricey ($100-$250 a night, single and double), but comparable in class to a hotel for the same rate. The rooms, all feature cable TV, wet bars, whirlpool baths, and terry-cloth robes. The guest receives a newspaper at the door every morning and a complimentary membership to the nearby Colony Square Athletic Club. Heartfield Manor, in historic Inman Park east of Atlanta, is a restored 1903 Tudor home with shingled, diamond-paned windows and beamed ceilings. The Manor has a single, a double and a suite available at very modest rates ($30, $40, $50). The suite has a refrigerator, microwave, bath and fireplace. Woodruff Bed and Breakfast is a Victorian home with a front porch and rocking chairs overlooking a wooded lawn. Rooms are decorated in 19th- and 20th-century antiques and feature stained-glass and bay windows. Rates are moderate: $65, $75 and $100 for singles, doubles, and two rooms with a common bath. All serve complimentary breakfast, ranging from continental to ham and eggs. For information about other B&B's, contact Bed & Breakfast Atlanta.

Ansley Inn, 253 Lafayette Dr.; (404) 892-2318. *Ansley Park*

Heartfield Manor, 182 Elizabeth St.; (404) 523-8633. *Inman Park*

Woodruff Bed and Breakfast, 223 Ponce de Leon Ave.; (404) 875-9449. *Midtown*

Bed & Breakfast Atlanta, (404) 875-0525. Office hours Monday-Friday 9:00 a.m.-noon, 2:00 p.m.-5:00 p.m.; outside of office hours, leave a voice-mail message.

89 / Calories? . . . Who Cares!

The Original Pancake House

Trying to lose weight? Want to lower your calorie and fat intake? Then, by all means avoid the Original Pancake House. This restaurant should bear a warning label from the Surgeon General. The Original Pancake House prides itself on serving heavy whipping cream with coffee and using the same blood-thickening agent in all its batters. The OPH isn't packed on Saturday and Sunday mornings for nothing. In addition to serving the city's best pancakes and fluffy omelets the size of small throw pillows (stuffed with everything from bacon and cheese to fresh asparagus), the restaurant offers breakfast items not offered elsewhere. The house-specialty Dutch Baby—a plate-sized, cupped crepe served with whipped butter, powdered sugar and fresh lemon wedges—alone is worth the trip. Pancakes come in 14 varieties, including sour dough, blueberry and Georgia pecan. The OPH also offers crepes in seven varieties. Our favorite: the Continental Crepe, stuffed with sour cream, laced with Cointreau and topped with maple syrup (100 percent pure maple syrup is available for additional cost). The restaurant serves a basic breakfast as well: eggs to order, grits, hash browns, toast, bacon, sausage or ham. Bagels and an assortment of fresh fruits are served as well. Atmosphere in the restaurant is nothing special: upholstered booths, butcher block tables, hard wooden chairs. On weekends there's a 15-30-minute wait. Service is spotty, especially during peak periods. The OPH has four Atlanta locations.

Brookhaven

The Original Pancake House, 4330 Peachtree Rd. N.E.; (404) 237-4116. Hours: Saturday and Sunday, 7:00 a.m.-4:00 p.m., Monday-Friday, 7:00 a.m.-3:00 p.m. No reservations.

90 / Contender on the Waterfront

Ray's on the River

Atlanta, believe it or not, is built on the banks of a river. Yet, the average visitor would never know that the Chattahoochee River flows through the western edge of the city because stringent environmental regulations have severely restricted development along its banks. Outside of canoeing, rafting, fishing or taking nature walks along the river in parks north of downtown, there are precious few places to partake of "The Hooch." One stands out: Ray's on the River, a 10-year-old restaurant and bar just inside the perimeter northwest of the city. Ray's offers a spectacular view of the Chattahoochee, which, on its best days looks pristine, clear, cold and shimmering. In the late afternoon, the view from Ray's glassed-in River Room is as picturesque as any sunset in the city. For years the restaurant's popularity has been hampered by so-so food. The recent hiring of Chop's former chef, Thomas Minchella, promises an upgrade with an emphasis on fresh seafood and first-rate steaks. Currently the menu's highlights include blackened Fish Alexander (fresh fish, type varying according to availability, seared with spices and topped with shrimp, scallops and Alexander sauce); lemon artichoke chicken; and a combination prime rib and salmon platter. The restaurant has a wide selection of wines and excellent desserts. Come early to get a table by the window overlooking the river. Request either the upstairs River Room, or downstairs patio seating, which is enclosed. A jazz/rock combo plays in the bar area Monday-Saturday, from 8 p.m. to midnight. Ray's is crowded on weekends.

Northwest

Rays on the River, 6700 Powers Ferry Rd.; (404) 955-1187. Hours: Lunch Monday-Saturday 11 a.m.-3:00 p.m.; Sunday 9:30 a.m.-3:30 p.m. Dinner: Monday-Thursday 5:30-10:30 p.m; Friday and Saturday 5:00 p.m.-12 midnight; Sunday 5-10:00 p.m.

91 / Roots in Atlanta

Auburn Avenue

Historically, Auburn Avenue is hallowed ground, the birth and resting place of Martin Luther King Jr., the site of his pulpit (Ebenezer Baptist Church) and the national headquarters of the Southern Christian Leadership Conference King helped found in 1957. Culturally, Auburn Avenue—known as "Sweet Auburn"—was significant as the backbone of the black community in Atlanta. In the late 19th and early 20th centuries Auburn Avenue was known as the "richest Negro street in the world." Into the 1950s, when Atlanta was segregated, Auburn Avenue was the economic hub of middle class Atlanta blacks who went to church here, shopped here, and partook of the most colorful nightlife in the city. Jazz greats Ray Charles and Dizzy Gillespie played clubs here. The section declined in the 1960s and 1970s and now is the object of restoration as a National Historic District encompassing 12 blocks around the Martin Luther King, Jr. Center for Nonviolent Social Change (449 Auburn Ave.). Begin your tour here. The King Center can consume a day itself. Walk east on Auburn, cross Boulevard to King's birthplace (501 Auburn Ave.). The Queen Anne-style home, built in 1894, is managed by the National Park Service, which conducts free 30-minute tours. Across the street a few doors south, the Bryant-Graves House (522 Auburn Av.), also with a Park Service tour, is worth a stop: It was the home of Rev. Peter James Brant, an editor of the newspaper *Voice of the Negro*. As you turn and head west toward downtown, key sights include: the Ebenezer Baptist Church (407 Auburn Ave.) where King and his father both were pastors; headquarters of the Southern Christian Leadership Conference (334 Auburn Ave.), and the Royal Peacock Club (186 Auburn Ave.), where jazz legends played.

92 / Look . . . Up in the Sky

The Flying Pig

They are called barbecue restaurants in some parts of the country, but if you cross the Mason-Dixon Line heading south, you look for a Bar-B-Q shack. The Flying Pig has that semi-run down and grungy look that signals great barbecue. It sits behind a liquor store off Virginia Avenue on the south side of Atlanta near the airport. Even if you miss the pig-with-wings sign, you can follow the unmistakable smell of hickory smoke. The place is not fancy or large. You can sit at the counter or at small, rickety tables, but it makes no difference once the food arrives. Ribs, coleslaw, Brunswick stew and other dishes are available, but make no mistake—the chopped pork sandwich is the way to go. This sandwich is full and fat and can be ordered on white bread or, more correctly for the professional pork eater, on a bun. A bag of chips and a large glass of sweet tea with one of these sandwiches will put you in hog heaven. The folks are friendly and the service is good. They are also accustomed to take out orders; you can run in wearing curlers or a sweatsuit and no one will bat an eye. If you only have time for one Bar-B-Q sandwich while in Atlanta, this is the one.

Out of Town

The Flying Pig, 856 Virginia Avenue, Hapeville, GA 30354; (404) 559-1000. Hours: Monday 10:30 a.m.-3:00 p.m., Tuesday-Friday 10:30 a.m.-8:00 p.m., Saturday 11:30 a.m.-8:00 p.m. Closed Sundays.

93 / Use Every Club in Your Bag

Golf Courses

Not too many years ago, Atlanta's only good golf courses were private clubs most people couldn't even get into by the back door. Public courses tended to resemble the beaches at Normandy—and some of them were just about as safe. But we're glad to report that today's Atlanta boasts some outstanding public courses. Here are some terrific choices.

Eagle Watch: This Arnold Palmer-designed course in considered one of the plums in the area. Located among rolling hills 45 minutes north of downtown. The Southerness: Finish this course and you'll want to come back and play again. The three finishing holes, all over or around a large lake, are outstanding; you can relax afterward with a cocktail on the verandah. Lake Spivey Golf Club: This 27-hole layout offers challenging golf for all levels of player; it's on the southside only 20 minutes from the airport. A good deal for the money, though sometimes crowded on weekends. Georgia National Golf Club: One of the newest, most demanding courses in the area, located 40 minutes south of downtown. Because of the hills and valleys, the course plays longer than its 6,874 yards. Better bring your boomstick. Rivers Edge: Short and tight in places, wide open in others, this is a course that will have you using every club in your bag. Located 30 minutes south of downtown.

Out of Town

Eagle Watch, 3055 Eagle Watch Drive, Woodstock, GA 30189; (404) 591-1000.

The Southerness, 4871 Flat Bridge Road, Stockbridge, GA 30281; (404) 808-6000.

Lake Spivey Golf Club, 8255 Club House Way, Jonesboro, GA 30236 (404) 477-9836.

Georgia National Golf Club, 1715 Lake Dow Road, McDonough, GA 30253; (404) 914-9994

Rivers Edge, 40 Southern Golf Court, Fayetteville, GA 30214; (404) 460-1098. Green fees range between $29 and $55, depending upon course and day of the week. Tee times are strongly recommended.

94 / Civil War High Point

Kennesaw Mountain/National Battlefield Park

The 2,882-acre park covers the site of what many regard as the Confederate high point in the Battle of Atlanta. As Union forces under the command of Major General William T. Sherman pushed south into Georgia in the summer of 1864 to lay siege to the city, they were met by strong resistance from Confederate troops under General Joseph E. Johnson. With Sherman's larger force advancing relentlessly, the Confederates retreated to fortified positions on Kennesaw Mountain, where, from the high ground with batteries of cannon, they inflicted heavy losses on Sherman's troops. The Confederates were never overrun, but this holding action did not save Atlanta. Sherman's troops skirted Kennesaw, the battle moved south, and Union forces eventually took the city. Today, Confederate entrenchments still scar the mountainside. Begin your tour of the battlefield at the Visitor Center at the foot of Kennesaw, where you can watch a slide show detailing the battle and view exhibits of Civil War artifacts. With a map available in the Center, visitors can take a self-guided tour. Some 16 miles of hiking trails criss-cross the mountain and surrounding terrain. The trail to the top is strenuous, so wear comfortable shoes and light clothing in warm weather. Hiking boots are not a bad idea. But the hike up is worth it. From the top, you get a panoramic view of Atlanta, and on clear days can see all the way to Stone Mountain. Even for non—Civil War buffs, Kennesaw is a wonderful day in the rough. Pack a lunch and enjoy the scenery. The best seasons are spring when the flowers are in bloom and autumn when the leaves are changing. For more.Civil War history, visit Big Shanty Museum, which is only a few miles away. Together, Kennesaw and Big Shanty will take an entire day to tour.

Out of Town

Kennesaw Mountain/National Battlefield Park, 900 Kennesaw Mountain Drive, Kennesaw, GA 30152; (404) 427-4686. Hours: seven days a week 8:30 a.m.-5:00 p.m. Admission is free.

95 / Country Two-Step

Country Music and Dancing

Country music, as much a part of the South as stock car racing and barbecue, is an orphan in Atlanta. Most of the places where boots and hats are formal evening wear and line dancing is an art form are not in the city. We think these are the best bets and they are worth the drive.

Miss Kitty's: Located 30 minutes north of downtown Atlanta, this is one of the most popular spots in the Atlanta area. This is a foot-stomping place offering a full-service restaurant and live music every night. There are big-screen televisions and pool tables if you just want to sip a cold one and pass the time. Miss Kitty's has a hotline providing information on the events of the day. Mama's Country Showplace: This mammoth nightspot 30 minutes east of the city is made for the dancer in you. The 2,000-square-foot dance floor can fill up on Saturday nights, and the regular house band will keep you moving. Food is limited to standard but acceptable bar fare, and prices are reasonable. Mama's will occasionally book big-name acts, so check the entertainment listings. Crystal Chandelier: Forty-five minutes north of Atlanta lies what may be the largest dance floor in the state—4,000 square feet. Guest bands provide the entertainment unless a major act has been booked. Sunday night is family night and no alcohol is served. *Out of Town*

Miss Kitty's, 1038 Franklin Road, Marietta, GA 30342; (404) 424-6556. Hours: Monday-Saturday 6:00 p.m.-2:00 a.m. Restaurant serves from 7:00-11:30 p.m. Closed Sundays. Admission: Monday-Thursday $3, Friday and Saturday $5.

Mama's Country Showplace, 3952 Covington Highway, Decatur, GA 30032; (404) 288-6262. Hours: Wednesday and Thursday 7:00 p.m.-1:00 a.m., Friday 7:00 p.m.-4:00 a.m., Saturday 7:00 p.m.-3:00 a.m. Admission: $5 cover charge.

Crystal Chandelier, 1750 North Robert Road. Kennesaw, GA 30144; (404) 426-5006. Hours: Wednesday-Friday 7:00 p.m.-2:00 a.m., Saturday 7:00 p.m.-3:00 a.m., Sunday 4:00-11:00 p.m. Closed Mondays and Tuesdays. On most nights the cover charge is $5; that changes occasionally if a big act is appearing.

96 / Where Duffers Go to Find the Answer

Old Sport Golf

If you are crazy about golf—and what golfer is not slightly crazy—then Old Sport Golf needs to be on your itinerary. This is not your standard golf shop but a treasure-trove of golf clubs, antiques and memorabilia. At any given time, there are from 30,000 to 40,000 golf clubs at Old Sport. Like any good golf shop, you can find the modern, state-of-the-art, graphite-shafted wonder club that will solve all your problems (except for the fact they all hit long in the store). However, what you can also find at Old Sport is that a vintage weapon may really be the answer. Even if you don't need any new clubs—though you can't be a serious golfer if you don't need at least one more stick—it's worth a stop at Old Sport to browse the classic club room. Some of the old clubs exhibited here will make you appreciate the playing ability of the old-timers. Also on display are some rare antiques and artwork that you might not see elsewhere, like a bust of Arnold Palmer that sells for $16,500. The people are friendly and you can browse without buying. They can also help you hunt down a special club and the trade-in system is alive well. *One note:* Golf is an expensive game and antiques and classic clubs are no exception. Depending upon their condition and nature, some items can be very expensive. But a visit here may also be educational: you might find out that old putter in the attic is worth a lot more than you thought. Old Sport is located on the north side of Atlanta and is easily reached off I-85.

Out of Town

Old Sport Golf, 4297 I-85 North Access Rd., Doraville, GA 30340; (404) 493-4344. Hours: Monday-Saturday, 10:00 a.m.-6:00 p.m.; Sunday, Noon-4:00 p.m. *Note:* Sunday hours are subject to change during winter so it's best to call.

97 / Where the "Great Locomotive Chase" Began

Big Shanty Museum

This is the site where the "Great Locomotive Chase" of the Civil War began. In April 1862, a Union spy and a group of northern soldiers dressed as civilians hijacked the locomotive engine General with the goal of running north and destroying tracks, bridges and telegraph lines behind them. The idea was to cut the supply routes from Virginia to Mississippi. Confederate troops discovered the theft, boarded the locomotive Texas and the first southern high speed pursuit was on. Running the Texas backwards up the tracks, the Confederates finally caught up with the General and the mission failed. The Big Shanty Museum exhibits Civil War artifacts, photographs and memorabilia related to the chase, with the major attraction being the locomotive "General" itself. Visitors can watch a video show narrating the highlights of the chase which is so storied it inspired a Disney movie, *The Great Locomotive Chase*. A gift shop is on the premises. Large groups can make reservations in advance. A history or Civil War buff should not miss this attraction; along with the Kennesaw Mountain/National Battlefield Park just a few miles away, it can be a full day. The other half of the chase, Texas, is on display at the Cyclorama. Some of the Union spies were buried at Oakland Cemetery (see separate listings for both).

Out of Town

Big Shanty Museum, 2829 Cherokee St., Kennesaw, GA 30152; (404) 427-2117. Hours: Monday-Saturday 9:30 a.m.-5:30 p.m., Sunday noon-5:30 p.m. Admission: adults $3, seniors $2.50, children $1.50, under seven free.

98 / The Family Amusement Park

Six Flags Over Georgia

Bring your children to Atlanta and don't visit Six Flags and you'll live to hear about it for years to come. The amusement park, one of the city's top attractions, has more than enough to offer children and adults. A day here and every sense will be sated. The park, 12 miles west of Atlanta and easily accessible off I-20, has more than 100 rides, including The Ninja, Mind Bender, and Scream Machine roller coasters. The first two combine enough spin-compressing loops, corkscrew turns, and plunging power dives to induce cowardice in a Kamikaze pilot. The Scream Machine is a classic old-style hair-raising wood-frame coaster, a replica of the Coney Island Cyclone. Other signature thrillers include the Great Gasp, a 20-story parachute jump that evokes the feeling of being shoved off a cliff and Thunder River, an ersatz Colorado River ride down swirling rapids. For smaller children and quieter souls other attractions include a riverboat ride, Ferris wheels, a merry-go-round, the Monster Plantation, bumper cars, a train ride, log flume, and many more. The park also has a huge video arcade, special themed stunt shows, a marine performance with dolphins and seals, and hourly song and dance performances, at the Crystal Pistol. The park features frequent headline concerts at the 8,000-seat Southern Star Amphitheater.

Out of Town

Six Flags Over Georgia, 7561 Six Flags Rd. S.W., Austell, GA 30001; (404) 948-9290. Hours: Open Daily from Memorial Day to late August, weekends only from early March to Memorial Day, and September through October 31. Gates open 10 a.m. Admission: adults $25, children ages 3 to 19 $18, senior citizens $14, children 2 and under free.

99 / Where the South Rises

Georgia's Stone Mountain Park

One of the Atlanta's most recognizable landmarks is actually 16 miles east of the city, but it's easily accessible by the Stone Mountain Freeway, which can be accessed off the I-285 perimeter highway or by taking Highway 78 (Ponce De Leon Avenue) from downtown. The giant gray granite monolith (the world's largest) is the centerpiece of a 3200-acre multirecreational facility that includes a 365-acre lake with a paddlewheel riverboat, a 36-hole Robert Trent Jones golf course, a 5-mile train ride around the mountain's base, and skylift cable car to the top (where an observatory offers a spectacular view of Atlanta to the west, and Kennesaw Mountain 30 miles to the northwest). The state-owned park offers more than enough sights and Civil War history to consume a full day. The highlight is the world's largest relief carving (90 feet high, 190 feet across), which took 50 years to complete. Conceived by Gutzon Borglum, who carved Mt. Rushmore, the carvings of Confederate President Jefferson Davis and generals Robert E. Lee and "Stonewall" Jackson are stunning. From April through Labor Day, the park puts on a spectacular nightly laser, fireworks and music show under the carving. Other points of interest include the Memorial Depot, an old-fashioned train station that houses a Civil War-era train and steam engine. Other attractions include the Antebellum Plantation, a 19-building evocation of pre-Civil War Georgia; the Antique Auto & Music Museum; and Stone Mountain Lake (site of several events during the 1996 Olympics), where park visitors can swim, rent boats, camp out and enjoy other activities.

Out of Town

Georgia's Stone Mountain Park, U.S. 78, Stone Mountain, GA 30086; (404) 498-5707. Hours: Sunday-Saturday, 6:00 a.m.-midnight. Admission: $5 for a one-day parking permit ($20 for a one-year pass); a ticket for all 6 major attractions is $12.50 for adults, $7.50 for children 3-11. Individual tickets range from $1.50-$3.00 each; children under 3 free.

100 / Wet 'n' Wild Attractions

White Water Park and/American Adventures Park

A downscale, much wetter version of Six Flags Over Georgia, White Water Park/American Adventures Park—adjacent theme parks owned by the same company—offer kids and adults who are young at heart a break from the heat and bustle of downtown but less hassle than a day-long venture to Six Flags or Stone Mountain Park. White Water, the Southeast's largest water-themed park, features two 400-foot enclosed water slides eerily illuminated with strobe lights. At the "Atlanta Ocean," a wave machine creates a continuous four-foot surf (bigger than you'll find in the Gulf of Mexico 9 days out of 10) in a 700,000-gallon pool. At Dragon Tail Falls, swimmers slide down a harrowing 250-food slide at speeds approaching 30 miles an hour. White Water features an array of other wet 'n' wild attractions and has special facilities for tots, all watched over by an army of 300-plus life guards. At American Adventures (which you might want to visit first), the major attraction is the Great Race, where you can put a gas-powered go-cart through its paces on a 1200-foot snaking track. Other highlights include a video and game arcade, bumper cars (drive like dad!), a classic carousel, tilt-o-whirl and miniature golf. Many visitors break their trip into two days. Be sure and pack swimming suits for White Water.

Out of Town

White Water Park/American Adventures Park, 250 North Cobb Parkway N.E. Marietta, GA 30062; (404) 424-9283. Hours: White Water is open weekends only in May and September and seven days a week from Memorial Day to Labor Day from 10:00 a.m. Closing times vary. American Adventures is open year-round, seven days a week. Hours vary seasonally. Admission: White Water: $15.50 adults, $9.50 for children 4, up to 4-feet tall; children under 4 and senior citizens, free. American Adventures: Free, you pay per ride; a $9.99 ticket for unlimited rides for children; $1.99 for adults.

101 / Talk to the Animals
Yellow River Wildlife Game Ranch

The 24-acre Yellow River game ranch offers the opportunity for you to have a close encounter of the animal kind. You can mingle among some 600 animals, including young offspring, with the opportunity to not only view but feed and pet them as well. Deer, rabbits, porcupines, goats, and a variety of other creatures roam this ranch. There is a herd of buffalo, supposedly the largest roaming herd east of the Mississippi River, and a skunk named William T. Sherman. (*Remember:* This is the South.) The most well-known resident is the groundhog, General Lee. While not as famous as his northern cousin, General Lee is a renowned weather forecaster. General Lee has a true understanding of southern weather patterns and if he comes out on February 2, Groundhog Day, you can count on six more weeks of winter. The animals here are accustomed to being around people and are not shy about nuzzling right up to you. Ranch workers can offer a lot of information about the various animals, and before you leave you will feel as if you've made a lot of new friends. This is a wonderful and educational place for children. Your best bets are to bring a picnic lunch and make a day of it. Wear comfortable shoes and dress appropriately for the weather. Although it is 45 minutes from downtown, it is really worth the drive. A gift shop is available.

Out of Town

Yellow River Wildlife Game Ranch, 4525 Highway 78, Lilburn, GA 30247; (404) 972-6643. Hours: seven days a week 9:30 a.m.-6:00 p.m.

Index